Navigating friendships as women can be difficult and confusing. Mary DeMuth has written an excellent guide—showing us how to avoid "deadly" traits in others while recognizing less-than life-giving traits in ourselves.

Joanna Weaver, author of *Having a Mary Heart in a Martha World*

Wouldn't it be the grandest thing to live in a world where we didn't need this book? That world is coming, but it ain't here yet! In the meantime, read this book first to make sure *you're* not one of these toxic "friends," and then read it to discern how to move forward (or away) from those who are.

Leslie Leyland Fields, speaker and author of several books, including *The Wonder Years*

In *The Seven Deadly Friendships*, Mary DeMuth puts words to the friendship grief we have all encountered. She gives us space to work through our unique situations as we feel seen and validated. If you want to be equipped to identify destructive friendship patterns and gain life-giving practices you can implement today, you need this book!

Melissa Spoelstra, speaker and author of *Elijah*

In 30 years as a mental health practitioner, I've had the privilege of working with patients who have struggled with and suffered through relationships akin to those detailed in *The Seven Deadly Friendships*. Mary helps us identify those toxic relationships and then points us to seven life-giving practices to help us receive and extend healthy friendships.

Dr. Michelle Bengtson, board certified clinical neuropsychologist, author of *Hope Prevails*

With warmth and candor, Mary DeMuth writes about deadly friendships in a life-giving way. Her "hard-won wisdom" will enlighten and encourage you to examine your own friendships. Everyone can benefit from this compelling book filled with scriptural truth and memorable stories that ultimately point to Jesus and the path to healing.

Judy Gordon Morrow, author of *The Listening Heart*

The Seven Deadly Friendships is a great addition to any counseling center's resource list. Our center will be recommending it often. Mary DeMuth not only accurately identifies numerous traits of difficult people but also gives practical solutions to those who are struggling.

Michelle Nietert, M.A., LPC-S, clinical ⟨...⟩ tes

Vulnerably sharing her own experience and that of countless others, Mary DeMuth points us toward finding and becoming healthy, whole friends. Learn how you can break free from shallow and toxic relationships, cultivating life-giving, joyful bonds instead.

Cherie Lowe, author of *Your Money, Your Marriage*

Mary DeMuth is a gentle, wise and humane guide to navigating those ruptures, healing wounds old and new, and confronting the messed-up patterns that caused us to choose those friendships in the first place. *The Seven Deadly Friendships* is a bracingly truthful and deeply graceful journey into the past and the present.

Lorilee Craker, author of 15 books, including *Anne of Green Gables, My Daughter and Me*

Like a traveler who found her way out of a dark valley, Mary DeMuth is a seasoned guide when it comes to navigating the rocky terrain of unhealthy friendships. Each chapter of *The Seven Deadly Friendships* is bursting with personality traits, character sketches, and personal examples that provide a detailed map of how to get out of the pit of friendship despair.

Anna LeBaron, author of *The Polygamist's Daughter*

As a faith-based counselor, I sit across from people day after day who have been harmed by those who pretended to mean them well. The end of a friendship is not only difficult to process, but it can be even more difficult to identify when an end is needed. Mary DeMuth comes to us with wisdom and depth on a subject many want to talk about but, until now, haven't had the right resource and tool.

Erin Kincaid, Higher Hopes Counseling founder, author of *Rock Me Right*

I found *The Seven Deadly Friendships* to be both challenging and encouraging as I applied Mary's heartfelt wisdom to my own relationships. Through personal stories and rare vulnerability, Mary helps us discover friendship traps to avoid, as well as find ways we can strengthen the relationships we treasure.

Rachel Anne Ridge, artist, speaker, and author of *Flash*

Having good, strong, godly friends has been a life-changer for me as I navigate motherhood and marriage. It takes work to be a good friend—and to have good friends—and Mary DeMuth's thoughtful, insightful and beautifully written guide gives great insight into not only the importance of friendship, but also how to build strong, lasting, godly, and life-changing friendships.

Erin MacPherson, author of *Put the Disciple into Discipline*

My heart is to always be a "safe" friend and to be aware of how to respond in a godly, healthy way when interacting with people with destructive motives or tendencies. Mary DeMuth gives hard-won insights and transparent vulnerability in sharing her personal experiences and research, providing a beautiful guide for forging ties that promote life.

Melinda Means, coauthor of *Mothering from Scratch*

Mary DeMuth is a "friend whisperer," and this book is filled with hard-earned insight and wisdom. Not only will you have stronger, deeper friendships as a result of reading it, but you'll *be* a better friend. You win and your friends do too.

Mary Byers, author of *How to Say No…And Live to Tell About It*

This book is a timely message that needs to get into the hands of men and women alike. I was challenged to evaluate myself and my friendships and to set healthy boundaries. *The Seven Deadly Friendships* is a book I will be giving as gifts and keeping as a resource in my own library!

Rachael Gilbert, speaker, blogger, podcaster, and cohost of the Declare Conference

Mary DeMuth provides an excellent tool to navigate some of the more difficult friendships with biblical wisdom, truth, and grace. *The Seven Deadly Friendships* helps provide a framework of awareness around some of the most toxic and destructive relationships we encounter.

Rev. Amy Graham, cofounder and pastor of spiritual care at The District Church, cofounder of DC127, and cofounder of the Boston Faith and Justice Network.

If you've ever found yourself staring at a trail of destruction left in the aftermath of a toxic relationship, wondering what just hit you, *The Seven Deadly Friendships* is for you. Mary DeMuth offers keen insights, hard-won wisdom, and—most importantly—a biblical perspective on the types of friendships that hurt us most and what to do about them.

Lindsay A. Franklin, bestselling author of *Adored*

I only wish *The Seven Deadly Friendships* had been written 20 years ago. Unfortunately, I relate all too well to many of the stories shared. But beyond being a practical primer of important warning signals, this book also offers heartfelt wisdom and biblical insight to navigate some of life's most difficult relational dynamics while preserving your own personal well-being in the process.

Michele Perry, brand strategist and coach for creatives, entrepreneurs and nonprofit leaders

What a great view into seven messy, and often common, unhealthy relationships! Not only does Mary describe character traits of potentially toxic friends, she also encourages the reader to look inward and examine their own heart and character for possibly damaging behavior toward others.

Elizabeth Welch, owner, PoppyLocks.com

Why would she do that? This tormenting question drove me to read *The Seven Deadly Friendships* in one sitting. Mary gives us answers, empathy, hope, and biblical help to move forward. This book is a must for every friend.

Lea Ann Garfias, author of three books, including *Rocking Ordinary*

Understanding the characteristics of the narcissist, the predator, the flake, and others helped me to let go of a portion of self-blame I'd been carrying as well as encouraged me to examine my own unhealthy contributions to friendships.

Ocieanna Fleiss, author of *Love Like There's No Tomorrow*

Once again, Mary DeMuth takes one for the team, fearlessly confronting an unavoidable topic. Masterfully written and easily understood, she offers hopeful advice, influenced by the truth of God's Word. You'll appreciate Mary's integrity and empathy interlaced through her candid, vulnerable, and bold style. No one is immune to a friend breakup; therefore, no one should be without this book.

Ellen Harbin, founder of the STAND women's conference and writer of the STAND Bible Study series

I wish I'd read this book years ago! Mary DeMuth provides a powerful tool in helping us recognize the warning signs *before* entering into a damaging friendship. A tool that could've informed my past relationships but will most definitely be applied to my future ones. *The Seven Deadly Friendships* belongs in every home— a resource you will refer to again and again!

T.H. Meyer, coauthor of *A God of All Seasons*

In an ocean of marriage and parenting books, Mary's voice is the still small whisper on an oft-overlooked area of heartache and confusion: friendship. Mary applies the seven deadly sins to friendship, helping the reader to identify and deal with those who might be narcissists, unreliable, predators, conmen, tempters, fakers, or dramatic. If you long to be a friend, have a friend, or understand friendship, this book is for you.

Amy Young, author of *Looming Transitions*

The Seven Deadly

Friendships

MARY DeMUTH

HARVEST HOUSE PUBLISHERS
EUGENE, OREGON

Cover Design and Illustration by Kyler Dougherty

Mary E. DeMuth is represented by David Van Diest from the Van Diest Literary Agency, 34947 SE Brooks Rd., Boring, OR 97009

The relational stories in this book originate from the author's experience and interviews. The names, identities, and circumstances have been altered and sometimes composited to protect privacy. Resemblance to actual individuals is coincidental and unintended.

The Seven Deadly Friendships
Copyright © 2018 Mary DeMuth
Published by Harvest House Publishers
Eugene, Oregon 97408
www.harvesthousepublishers.com

ISBN 978-0-7369-7486-8 (pbk)
ISBN 978-0-7369-7487-5 (eBook)

Library of Congress Cataloging-in-Publication Data
Names: DeMuth, Mary E., 1967- author.
Title: The seven deadly friendships / Mary DeMuth.
Description: Eugene, Oregon : Harvest House Publishers, 2018.
Identifiers: LCCN 2018000636 (print) | LCCN 2018021180 (ebook) | ISBN
    9780736974875 (ebook) | ISBN 9780736974868 (pbk.)
Subjects: LCSH: Friendship--Religious aspects--Christianity. | Deadly sins.
Classification: LCC BV4647.F7 (ebook) | LCC BV4647.F7 D46 2018 (print) | DDC
    241/.6762--dc23
LC record available at https://lccn.loc.gov/2018000636

Printed in the United States of America

18 19 20 21 22 23 24 25 26 / VP-SK / 10 9 8 7 6 5 4 3 2 1

To Heidi VanDyken

a faithful, kindhearted, truth-telling,
encourager of a friend who loves Jesus well
and demonstrates his love in a hundred
different, nonsplashy (but beautiful) ways.

Oh, how I adore you and treasure
our long-standing friendship!

Contents

WHY YOU NEED THIS BOOK

When I look back over my life, I recount it in stories, and those stories always involve relational snapshots. I've had the privilege of encountering some amazing friends over the years; they outweigh the more difficult relationships I've walked through, thankfully. But it's in the sting of pain in the aftermath of those broken circles that I reel. I rethink. I regrieve. I revisit. This past year has had its fill of devolving friendships, and I find myself introspecting to obsession, wondering how I could have prevented so much pain.

That journey informs every fiber of this book. As I've looked back, studied Scripture, prayed, and sought counsel, the Lord has graciously uncovered patterns—types of friends I've pursued who have not been good for me. And in that discovery, I realized you might appreciate these revelations too. I didn't create these categories, nor did I discern them over the years. It's taken decades for me to come to this place of settled "aha." I pray I can prevent your foray into destructive relationships through the pages of this book.

You may be familiar with the seven deadly sins. In the fourth century, a monk named Evagrius Ponticus created a list of eight. Later, in AD 590, Pope Gregory combined a few, added envy, and the list stuck even to our modern day: lust, gluttony, greed, sloth, wrath, envy, and pride.[1] Although a solidly historical list, I wanted to explore the biblical list of sins found in Proverbs 6:16-19:

> There are six things the LORD hates—
> no, seven things he detests:
> haughty eyes,
> a lying tongue,
> hands that kill the innocent,
> a heart that plots evil,
> feet that race to do wrong,
> a false witness who pours out lies,
> a person who sows discord in a family.

These seven traits correspond to the seven deadly friendships we sometimes find ourselves entangled in:

- One. "Haughty eyes" relates to our narcissistic friends.

- Two. "A lying tongue" points to our unreliable friends.

- Three. "Hands that kill the innocent" embodies our predatory friends.

- Four. "A heart that plots evil" correlates to our conman/woman friends.

- Five. "Feet that race to do wrong" are our tempter friends.

- Six. "A false witness" corresponds to our faker friends.

- Seven. "A person who sows discord" resembles our dramatic friends.

Chances are you've encountered one of these deadly friends in your life, which is why you've picked up this book. You, like me, have wrestled with why you allowed someone like that into your life, or you don't have enough editorial distance, and you continually blame yourself for someone else's bad behavior. You may be living in the land of "if only."

If only my narcissist friend would take the focus off himself for a moment, or allow me to share my pain so I could feel the joy of being loved by a narcissist. (Of course, this is an impossibility, but we still seem to think a narcissist can love us.)

If only my unreliable friend could be depended upon when my life breaks.

If only my predator friend could empathize, seeing things from my perspective so I could prove I can befriend anyone, even those who seem beyond rehabilitation.

If only my conman friend would stop to see me as a person, not a commodity to steal from.

If only my tempter friend could love me for who I am, accepting my desire to stay close to Jesus despite the heartache, but he only accepts me when I join his rebellion.

If only my faker friend would finally be real and let me into her life, but she can't seem to do that, enslaved to her addiction to situational ethics.

If only my dramatic friend could stop seeing himself as the center of the world long enough to acknowledge my needs and fears.

The problem with the land of "if only" is rarely do we migrate to the future. Seldom do we reach the relational nirvana we long for. We may spend years in friendship reformation projects, bending over backward in the hopes of seeing new light, but instead we stumble in darkness. Why? Because of this simple truth we know, but we forget: We cannot change people. We can only change ourselves—with God's beautiful help.

Before I go further, let me say that we also can be these types of friends. So I'm not writing this with the assumption that every person who reads this book is innocent, and every person "out there" is deadly. We're all an amalgamation of mess. Like you, I've experienced a number of broken friendships over the years, and often these painful breakups have harmed me, sucked dry my resolve to involve myself in other people's lives, and pushed me closer to cynicism—particularly when I realized I tended to chase these unsafe people. The pattern, in retrospect, is stunning. But I've also *been* some of these friends. I've had to be the one to apologize, to look at my own life and see where I've been toxic to someone else.

What if we could discover together our own faulty patterns, the *why* behind our pursuit of the unsafe? What if we could discern who might be predatory? What if we could look honestly at our relationships and figure out which ones deeply bless us and which ones drain us? How can we discern our own relational stew to discover what ingredients poisoned it and why? I hope to answer these questions—to illuminate the whys behind problematic friendships while also offering a way to walk through and heal from them. Some will heal and be reconciled, some will gradually die a mutually desired death, and some will disintegrate. And through it all, we always have the opportunity to grow spiritually. Because relational discord isn't always about our hurt—it's about our journey toward spiritual health.

But there are times we have to sever. We have to learn from past relationships so we can move forward with the new ones God has for us. Yet many of us stay entrenched in broken friendships for years and years because we can't see our patterns. We are terrified of change, worried about hurting someone else's feelings, or somehow feel we deserve harsh treatment. We worship the status quo.

Yet growth comes in endings.

"When we fail to end things well, we are destined to repeat the mistakes that keep us from moving on. We choose the same kind of dysfunctional person or demoralizing job again," author Henry Cloud writes. "Not learning our lessons and proactively dealing with them, we make the same business or personal mistakes over and over. Learning how to do an ending well and how to metabolize the experience allows us to move beyond patterns of behavior that may have tripped us up in the past. We do not have to keep repeating the same patterns."[2] But so many of us do. We chase deadly friendships with a clinging tenacity, hoping beyond hope that this time will be different.

Except it never is.

These deep friendships wound us; it is a universal truth. David experienced it too, often in the form of long-term betrayal. "This isn't the neighborhood bully mocking me—I could take that. This isn't a foreign devil spitting invective—I could tune that out. It's you! We grew up together! *You!* My best friend! Those long hours of leisure as we walked arm in arm, God a third party to our conversation" (Psalm 55:12-14 MSG).

Can you sense the agony in David's cadence? The sting of dismissal? The bewilderment? I've been there, and I've listened to enough stories to know that you've been there too. Particularly when a deadly friend erupts in anger—via conflict, misunderstanding, or differences in perspective. Harmony and companionship you thought were givens suddenly morph overnight into discord and hostility. I still feel the whiplash of the swift U-turns some of my friendships have taken.

And one haunts me nearly every day of my life—a mixture of narcissistic, unreliable, and predatory. Only now do I see this. Only now do I discern the patterns.

"I thought about her again," I tell my husband, Patrick, in the comfort of our living room.

He shakes his head. "Why do you do this to yourself?"

I shake my head too, mostly to loosen the memory of her, of the regrets and pain that remain quite alive between us. "What else could I have done?"

"You need to let it go, Mary. It's over. She's moved on. You need to too." He pats the couch, asks me to sit.

I do. "But I can't. I keep rehearsing what went wrong, what happened between us. We were supposed to be friends forever." I say the last word and think of the song Michael W. Smith crooned right around the time I graduated high school about friends being friends forever, if they share the same Lord. Why couldn't that be true?

I know Patrick wants to deliver me of this tenacious need to deconstruct every fallen relationship, but he remains blessedly silent. He reaches out and grabs my hand. And I sit there with a mind full of friendship memories that don't seem to have a proper place to live and move. They're floating untethered, no relationship to anchor them. They flash in and through me like flickering movies—bright splashes of laughter and shared motherhood, deep talks and tears of relief, bearing burdens and buying blouses, praying big kingdom prayers and recounting funny stories. But then other memories interrupt the flickering happiness—angry words and volatile misunderstandings, phone calls laced with pain and accusations of betrayal, final words and curt goodbyes.

Normally, I have words to describe how I feel. But in this moment, I have none. What's left is undecorated grief—as long as the friendship was deep.

As a society we've come to recognize divorce as a terrible scar. We agonize with widows and widowers and the loss of a significant, compelling relationship. But seldom do we put words to the grief of a friendship gone south. Sure, we talk about it with our remaining friends (or a long-suffering spouse in my case), but we almost feel like we don't have the right to grieve what we've lost. We justify that it's no big deal, and that we should get over it, for crying out loud. (And we do cry out loud, don't we?)

I asked my Facebook friends how they felt about their own deadly friendships. Two things emerged. One: I realized I was not alone in this type of grief. And two: So many struggle with this.

Lana writes about the hole left behind. "When it's a friend you've been very close to, it's hard for lots of reasons. There's a hole in your life that they used to fill—time, conversations, laughter…all the things you used to share with that person. People are not fungible; one friend can't be replaced with another. In addition, if you've been close, you've made yourself vulnerable to that person. You've let them see the real you, even the ugly parts, and if the 'breakup' was an unpleasant one, you now have someone out there that you trusted enough to confide in, but whom you can no longer trust to have your back."

Martina addresses the questions that so many of us ask when a friendship ends. "The betrayal, the fear of more hurt, the emptiness left behind, all of that takes time to work through and move past. I sometimes feel shame too. Why did I cause this friend to suddenly hate me? How did I hurt *them* that they felt they needed to leave? Why couldn't I better communicate my love and commitment to them in a way they understood? When my friends leave me, I'm left with the love I still have for them. And it hurts that I can't give that love to them in a way they can accept. I feel like I'm throwing my heart at a brick wall."

Cyndi adds to Lana's perspective about the vulnerability we experience after a relationship ends. After all, that friend knew deep secrets and parts of us we never shared with anyone else. She writes, "The vulnerability is the hardest part. Because now there is a part of you that not only regrets opening up to that person and allowing them to really, deeply know you, but you also worry that sharing so deeply could have been the very thing, that made them not want you in their life."

Let me just say this: I hear you. Your pain is real, and it is valid. You are not alone. Like Lana, Martina, and Cyndi, we all walk a difficult path when a friendship is broken. We all feel the hole left behind—even when the friend was deadly to our soul. We banter back and forth in our minds about what went wrong, hoping that if we could just process it perfectly, we could figure out how to fix it. Instead, we're left with a vulnerability hangover, feeling raw, used, and very, very tired.

The Seven Deadly Friendships is the book I needed to read when I sifted through the broken pieces of friendships gone awry. I pray that it puts words to the grief, adds context to the mayhem, and provides you with the space you need to process a difficult relationship. But more than that, I hope to put words to why those relationships failed in the first place—why you pursued them, and why they might not have been healthy in the first place.

I am, unfortunately, not a relationship expert, nor am I credentialed in counseling. But I have walked some deep waters through broken friendships, and I have experienced God's nearness in the midst of that mess. I'm not writing a clinical book dissecting the minutiae of relationships and detailing the latest research on codependency (though I will cite sources that I find helpful). I'm writing a ripped-from-the-headlines companion guide—of my own life and the lives of those with whom I've had the pleasure of interacting around this topic. This is an I've-been-there-and-survived-and-learned-a-few-things tome where my main objective is to help you feel seen and validated.

This book is based on the reality of your pain—you are not alone, and you are not crazy—and it's based on Scripture, namely the Proverbs verses above and the lives of two important biblical figures: Joseph and Jesus. The Proverbs verses unpack and define the deadly friends, while looking at Joseph and Jesus in the second half of the book will help us reconstruct a wisdom-based paradigm—a new way forward as we navigate new, healthy relationships.

For ease of discussion, I've decided to name these deadly friendships, each one with its own chapter. Apologies ahead of time if one of them is your name: Narcissist Nolan, Unreliable Uma, Predator Paige, Conman Connor, Tempter Trevor, Faker Fiona, and Dramatic Drake.

Some of our broken friendships are a combination of these types of friends, and some defy categorization. But I've walked this world long enough to know (at least in my own experience) that our world is full of broken people, and sometimes those broken people break us.

This book is my gift to you—full of hard-won grief work, a resettled perspective, and wisdom like my husband's about letting go. But it's more than just a manual about pursuing healthy relationships, learning from the hard ones, and moving on. It's a book about all relationships, including your friendship with the eternal God who loves you. Jesus said we are to love God and love others. But so often others and their faulty ways of loving us become the catalyst that pushes us away from God. In short, people injure us, and that injury causes us to doubt the goodness of God. So our injury becomes twofold: between others and between our Creator and us.

I believe that you'll not only close this book wiser and more discerning, but that the book will serve as an inauguration toward personal revival. As you navigate your relationships and experience healing, it's my prayer that your affection for the Almighty—the relational God who initiates community—will increase.

Frederick Buechner confirms this correlation:

> Maybe nothing is more important than that we keep track, you and I, of these stories of who we are and where we have come from and the people we have met along the way because it is precisely through these stories in all their particularity, as I have long believed and often said, that God becomes known to each of us most powerfully and personally. If this is true, it means to lose track of our stories is to be profoundly impoverished not only humanly but also spiritually.[3]

This book is the tracking of our relational stories. It's a place to evaluate, discern, and move on. And as we do, we begin to see the beauty of God materialize before us. It's his pursuit of us when we're bleeding and broken that helps us heal in the aftermath. It's his affection for us when we lick our wounds and hurt deeply that reminds us he understands.

After all, Jesus was betrayed by a friend—a close friend. He experienced every kind of deadly friend, and because he has walked painful friendship paths, he knows how to comfort us when we grieve, and he empowers us when we choose to move on. He is our best friend, the safest one, who knows our secret fears and doesn't betray them. He embodies Proverbs 27:9, "The heartfelt counsel of a friend is as sweet as perfume and incense."

I've often shared, "What wounds us is what heals us," meaning if we are wounded in bad community, the way back to health is good community. Jesus is the best community, capable of healing your tender heart. He will help you discern who to pursue, when to pull back, and when it's wise to move on. And through all that, my prayer is that you will find him close by. After all, Psalm 34:18 reminds us: "The Lord is close to the brokenhearted; he rescues those whose spirits are crushed."

I would be remiss if I didn't continue to mention that we can also be deadly friends. All of us have traits of these folks lurking in our heart, so at the end of every chapter, I ask some questions to help you discern if you are harming someone else in your friendships. It's also instructive to remember that the people you find the most fault in, the ones who drive you the craziest, are often those who struggle with the same relational sins you do. For instance, I tend to be pretty judgmental of the Dramatic Drakes of my life. That instant ire serves as a window to my soul because I struggle with giving in to drama. This realization and self-awareness helps me do two things: to be kind to Dramatic Drake, and to use my frustration not as a means to help him be better, but to turn the spotlight onto myself and consider how I can grow in this area.

That's why I don't want you to miss the last chapter of this book. It crystallizes all I've been learning about recovery and abundance in the midst of difficult relationships. It's the counteractive ingredient to seven deadly friendships—the seven life-giving practices you can implement today, regardless of the current state of your relationships. It's steeped in hard-won truth based on years of making relational mistakes, coaching others in difficult relationships, and reading a ton of books.

My hunch is that you picked up this book because of a crushed spirit. Someone you thought would be there forever, a friend who morphed from ally to adversary, has wounded you. You're living in the pain of that betrayal, and you want to make sense of it all, learn from it, and find healing. So before you turn the page to chapter 1, where we dive headlong into the first deadly friendship, do you mind if I pray for you?

Jesus, I pray for my friend reading these words today. Would you shoulder the grief? Would you gently remind that you completely understand what it's like to walk through betrayal? Please comfort, heal, and establish. Bring a new perspective and a holy understanding of what it means to engage in a world that hurts you. Oh, how we all need you, Jesus. Without you, we are crushed. With you, we are loved. Holy Spirit, please illuminate the journey my friend will take to assess current and past friendships. Amen.

Part One

The Deadly Friendships

Narcissist Nolan

"Haughty Eyes"

|t was her eyes. How they narrowed when she said the words that confounded me.

"I don't understand why Jesus would die for me," she said, a smile playing on her lips. We sat in a restaurant while others lunched. I picked at a hangnail, wondering how this line of reasoning would play out.

"I know. It's hard to believe," I said. Jesus had forgiven me of so much, and I was well aware that the balance of my sins compared to a holy God didn't make sense, thanks to grace.

"No," she said. "I understand why Jesus died for you." Those eyes bored into my insecurity. The Mona Lisa smile remained. Then she lifted her chin and landed her gaze on an unsuspecting diner. "And that guy over there. I know why Jesus died for him. He sins."

I took a bite.

"You see, I don't really sin. So why would Jesus have to die for me?"

I didn't have a reaction for my friend in that moment, other than wanting to move my chair away from the possible lightning strike. Researchers tell us we have three typical responses when we encounter something unexpected: fight, flee, or freeze. Me? I freeze. The words came a few hours later, but in that moment, silence. But her words sent me researching, and in that quest, I discovered something that would change my life.

Narcissists.

If you've been raised by one (or two), you'll spend your life trying to resolve a painful puzzle: performing all sorts of emotional gymnastics to make a narcissist love you. The problem is this: Narcissistic people are incapable of empathy, other-centered love, or healthy relationships. Yet, we chase. Just like I chased my friend who seemed to think she never sinned.

So who is Narcissist Nolan? What makes him tick? Why is he the way he is? Before we delve into folks like this, there's an important distinction to make. There's a difference between a person with narcissistic tendencies and someone who has Narcissistic Personality Disorder. The difference is in the degree of pain they inflict (from a molehill to a mountain) and their ability to change (from a little to none at all). Either way, there's a reason Narcissist Nolan is the way he is, typically because of a lack of personal attachment in childhood. And this lack has followed him into adulthood, manifesting itself in several different ways.

Traits

Narcissist Nolan behaves this way:

- Like Narcissus (whom this trait is named after), he must have constant attention, be told often of his positive attributes, and be heralded exclusively.

- He has a keen sense of grandiosity, as if he is uniquely special. He spends an inordinate amount of time talking about himself, his unique characteristics, great accomplishments, and his heroic ability to take care of everyone.

* He is extremely jealous of anything that shows he is smaller, less important. And he is jealous of your time. He wants it all.

* He demands special treatment—from you, others, businesses, etc.

* Oddly, he is also extremely insecure, but he doesn't let on. Instead, he projects his insecurity onto others. He spends a lot of effort demeaning others, making them feel small and stupid.

* He cannot recount his childhood in vivid memories. Everything is vague.

* He completely lacks empathy. If you are hurting, it's your fault. He will not enter into your hurt. But he will go on and on about how you hurt him, or how the world has given him a raw deal.

* He takes credit for other people's accomplishments, including yours.

* He is an expert in gaslighting. In other words, he may say something that you know you heard, but when you bring that up, he looks at you like you're crazy. "I never said that" is the constant refrain of a narcissist. He does this to manipulate and control you, to make you unstable and crazy feeling. (The term comes from the 1944 movie *Gaslight*, where a husband systematically makes his wife think she's going crazy by altering the level of light in their home but telling her nothing has changed.)

- He cannot ever admit he's wrong. It's always someone else's fault, particularly yours.

- He cuts in line and doesn't care.

- He exaggerates.

- He can be passive-aggressive.

- He is overly sensitive and cannot take a joke.

- He is obsessed with himself. He is his own favorite subject. In order to have a long conversation, you have to steer the entire conversation to him. You sometimes grow exhausted trying to think up new questions to ask him.

- He must have the best of everything—the best opinion, the perfect car, the right kind of computer, and the most beautiful pet.

- He talks big, but his actions don't line up with his assertions.

- He changes the subject when emotions or feelings enter into a conversation.

- He is typically extremely intelligent, and he loves to let others know how sub-intelligent they are.

- He often contradicts himself, sometimes in the same breath. And he pretends the contradiction was your imagination.

- He is often envious of others and cannot stand to lose.

- He is easily cruel. Harsh words flow from him as if they'll carry no pain. Then he belittles you for being hurt. "You're overly sensitive," he'll say.

- He preys on those he perceives are his subordinates, but sucks up to anyone he sees as superior. He is well versed in flattery. He makes those "higher" than him an idol.

- He must be in control, and he must control you. Anytime you step outside of his wishes, you will be punished.

- He likes to dole out advice, even when it's not solicited.

- He doesn't like to hear about your preferences. And you've learned to never share what you want because the consequences of being honest this way are too severe.

- He gives contradictory gifts. He may ask you what you want but then give you the opposite gift and expect you to be ecstatic.

- He doesn't have a normal conscience and is only concerned about his reputation. If something tarnishes his position in the world, then he's more self-aware, but only in terms of damage control.

- He runs through relationships, demonizing the past ones, idealizing the present ones. As he gets to retirement age, he has typically cycled through all his relationships and faces being alone. (People have figured him out, and his circle shrinks.)

- He kicks you when you're down and has no empathy as he does so.

- He has the emotional intelligence of a child. He cannot read social cues.

- He flat out cannot hear any sort of criticism. He will instead retaliate and demean anyone who brings up an issue. In short, you will regret bringing up his shortcomings.

- He has manic swings—moving from wildly popular in public to condescending and demeaning in private.

- He loves to target codependent people.

- He is the master of triangulation, where he discloses bad parts of your relationship with others, even publicly on social media. He does this to keep control.

- He sees nothing wrong with interrupting you or others.

- He tells stories about himself where he is either the supreme hero or the extreme victim.

- He loves to use guilt to get you to comply.

- He often has "harems" of people surrounding him, so he has a constant source of affirmation.

- He lives entitled, as if everyone out there in the world owes him a perfect life, a perfect response, a perfect gift.

- Initially, he made you feel entirely amazing and wanted, only to shape-shift and turn on you. This is called idealization (or the "love-bombing" phase), the devaluation phase (where he undermines you constantly but throws in a few compliments, giving you hope that you'll return to the idealization phase), followed by the discard phase, where he abandons, then demonizes you.[1]

- He takes offense easily and tends to nurse grudges.

- If you walk away, you will become the "abuser," in his eyes, and he will slander you mercilessly.

- He exaggerates his talents, accomplishments, and successes (even if he doesn't have any of these things).

- He gets easily angered when he doesn't receive special treatment.

- He hates standing in line.

- He changes personalities to fit different situations.

- He makes excuses, but never owns his mistakes.

- He won't allow a bad picture of himself posted on social media.

- He has no idea he's a narcissist.

- He has the uncanny ability to get you to share your deepest thoughts, but he never returns the favor. This keeps him in power.

- He may confound you because although he's narcissistic, he actually might be introverted.

- He name-drops.

- He uses others to bolster his self-esteem—people (you!) are simply a projection of his ego.

- He is more interested in his perfect persona than being an authentic, vulnerable person.

- He hates your boundaries and violates them at will.

- He seems to be unconcerned that his actions have consequences.

- He is charming and flirtatious in public but an entirely different person behind closed doors. This is why it's hard to convince others of his dark side. Out in the world, he appears to be convivial and the life of the party.

- He constantly complains—particularly about you and your bad traits.

- He dehumanizes others and you.

- He blames you when he overreacts: "I wouldn't have to yell if you weren't so idiotic."

- He typically does not initiate in a relationship. You are responsible for everything moving forward.

- He sees himself as an archetype, a hero for the hour, and in Christian realms, as the ideal Christian.

- He uses language like "I told you so."

- He is (or perceives himself to be) very attractive.

- He doesn't care if he makes you late.

- He dominates conversations and talks exclusively about himself.

- He is preoccupied with success and nice things.[2]

THE LYING PASTOR

Tyler and Elizabeth both befriended a narcissistic man who also happened to be their pastor. At first everything went smoothly. They had recently relocated to a new city and struggled with the transition. Their life bent toward upheaval and a feeling of being untethered, except for their church—an anchor in the chaos. Sure, their pastor dismissed people and said unkind things from the pulpit (like demeaning people with emotional struggles), but no one was perfect, right?

Later, it was discovered that the pastor had stolen every single sermon he preached from the Internet, and, of course, lied about it. Not one sermon had been the result of study, prayer, or preparation. All had been reenacted word for word from other pastors' online sermons. The fallout? It took some time to uncover everything that had happened, but eventually the church leaders asked the pastor to step down. In his vacancy, a congregation battled questions, anger, and bewilderment. The pastor had been so charismatic, so funny, so mesmerizing. He seemed so on fire. But soon folks realized it had all been a farce—the carefully constructed image of a narcissistic man.

Most of what Tyler has learned blossomed in retrospect. "Narcissists remind me of the devil," he said. "He is smart enough to not manifest as all evil. He always adds sugar. Likewise, narcissists don't punch you in the face. Instead, they put their arm around you. The problem is, you don't realize that the other arm is stealing from you."

As he looked back, he realized this man hadn't actually been his friend. In fact, when the pastor talked to his closest friends after he was caught, he often said, "We didn't really have a friendship." Tyler admitted, "I was just a game piece. People turned out to be pawns in the chessboard of his life, and it was all about him winning."

In my own interaction with a particular narcissist (not the one mentioned at the beginning of this chapter), I realize, too, that I was only in relationship as long as it served the narcissist. Once I was no longer needed, she discarded me. What confounded me was trying to share my dismissal and pain with people who knew the narcissistic person in public. They only knew the charismatic, fun person and had a hard time believing I told the truth. People with this tendency are smart. They know when to act appropriately and when they can get away with demeaning behavior. In short: In public, they shine; in private, they violate.

Tyler shares this same observation. "He seemed like such a great guy. He seemed normal. Just like an apple looks normal until you take a bite, and it's rotten inside."

He and Elizabeth both found it difficult to understand a narcissist. "It was hard to get into his head. *Certainly, he can't be that sick,* we thought. It was hard to empathize with his lack of empathy." This is perhaps the hardest part for normal folks to understand. We try to empathize with someone who cannot seem to garner empathy. We invent stories of their past to try to justify or make sense of their lack of care for others.

Lily Hope Lucario wrote these highly instructive words: "Hurt people hurt people? Actually there are many traumatized and abused people who don't hurt people. They have compassion, empathy, a conscience, and would never want to hurt someone intentionally because they never want to inflict pain on anyone else. Being hurt is not an excuse for hurting others. Hurting people is a choice."[3] The problem is this: Some people don't have a reason or a why for their behavior. They simply cannot think of anyone other than themselves, and they spend their lives weaving stories that make them the hero or the victim.

Tyler likened the behavior of a narcissist to what grocery store managers call Quick Changers. They'll ask for change for a fifty, and then continue to ask for different denominations until they end up flustering the clerk, and they receive far more than they gave initially. It's supposed to be an even exchange, but it ends up not being one. Why? Because narcissistic people take more than they give, and they use flustering tactics to do so—usually making you feel crazy afterward, asking things like, "Did that just happen?" Tyler says the store management instructed its cashiers to stop immediately when they encountered a Quick Changer. "Don't play the game; you will lose. They are professionals. Stop the exchange," Tyler said. When he encountered yet another lie from the pastor, he employed this technique. He simply stopped him and said, "I don't believe what you just said to me."

Tyler now believes he stayed in the relationship (before terminating it permanently) because of his own savior complex. He thought he could fix the pastor. He now reflects, "Maybe Jesus can, but only if he lets Jesus fix him. I'm not going to be the one who fixes him. I can pray for him. I sincerely want him to be healthy, but I cannot be in a relationship with him."

Elizabeth was surprised at how deep and wide the pain spread to her, how all-encompassing it felt. "Because the situation was so extreme, I feel like it was all consuming in my mind. I was surprised how psychologically damaging it was. I reeled trying to reconcile the man we knew with what had transpired. Now I know he was a calculating psychopath, and the emotional toll was shocking."

A few things she learned after the pastor's Internet sermon-stealing came to light began with something simple. "Don't excuse bad behavior or words. If there's a red flag, accept it. Don't overlook it." She also cautions people to realize when they're vulnerable. "Abusers prey on vulnerable people," she said. It is also important to ask yourself this question: "Am I putting up with this behavior because I'm in a lonely spot?"

She also cautions us to check our pride. Often narcissistic people thrive in positions of power, fame, or wealth. Because you might want to associate with such popular people, you may overlook some glaring problems. "You feel that pull toward their position. So you spend time with them, not necessarily because you like them, but because of their position. It's important to check your motives."

Tyler shares the cycle of grief he and Elizabeth walked through. "I started out sad. Sad for the pastor. Then confused. Then angry. Then I prayed for him—for repentance, to return to Jesus." But Tyler did not continue in a relationship with the pastor.

WHAT THE BIBLE SAYS

The Bible is chock full of character studies of people with narcissistic traits. When Satan tempted Adam and Eve, he appealed to their pride and desire for control. The moment sin entered the world, this preoccupation with self flourished. While writing this book, I've been on a two-month quest to read the entire Bible in chronological order. What stood out to me was how many times narcissistic people got into trouble, hurt people, and continued to do so. Reading about the era of kings cemented hopelessness in this regard. Because of sin, we will battle self-centeredness our whole lives. But because of Jesus and his beautiful intersection in our lives (and the outrageous gift of the Holy Spirit within us), we no longer have to be enslaved to narcissism.

But what happens when we encounter an entrenched narcissist? Paul writes starkly of their traits in 2 Timothy 3:1-5. Take special note of what he encourages our response to be at the end of the verses.

> You should know this, Timothy, that in the last days there will be very difficult times. For people will love only themselves and their money. They will be boastful and proud, scoffing at God, disobedient to their parents, and ungrateful. They will consider nothing sacred. They will be unloving and unforgiving; they will slander others and have no self-control. They will be cruel and hate what is good. They will betray their friends, be reckless, be puffed up with pride, and love pleasure rather than God. They will act religious, but they will reject the power that could make them godly. Stay away from people like that!

Like Tyler and Elizabeth decided to do, it's typically best to sever relationship with a narcissist—to stay away.

Why? We do this for the sake of potential reconciliation later. The truth is, narcissists can only love and worship themselves; therefore, they will continue to harm you as they elevate themselves. As long as you continue to be harmed, your injury will continually grow worse. Their continued attacks will only cause it to seep and fester. Best to first let the wound heal without further damage before you even entertain jumping back in.

But here's the sad truth: Most narcissistic people do not reform. I recently recounted a relationship I had with a narcissist that I naively thought had improved. But as I unpacked my story, I realized that the narcissistic person only used me when she needed my emotional support during a difficult trial. The moment she was back on her feet emotionally, she dismissed me and continued to betray—even worse than before. I forgot to examine the fruit of her life. Like Elizabeth, I dismissed her narcissistic traits, hoping beyond hope that she had finally changed. Initially, she covered up her narcissism for a period of time, but it reared its selfish head soon enough.

Clarissa didn't realize she married a narcissist, but she said something telling regarding expectations, something we must learn to manage. "I was in love with his potential." She went on to say that she didn't love who he was in the moment, but she engaged in what psychologists call "magical thinking," hoping that she could reform him. Instead, he violated her trust, pursued another woman, and broke her heart. Her only recourse was to separate herself from him. If you're in love with a friend's potential, but that person never seems to realize it, consider that a red flag. Heed Paul's warning to stay away or move away.

The best way to think logically about someone enslaved to narcissism is to look at his or her fruit. Jesus said, "You can identify them by their fruit, that is, by the way they act. Can you pick grapes from thornbushes, or figs from thistles?" (Matthew 7:16). Even by looking at a narcissist and their fruit, we have to be cautious and discerning.

My friend Jimmy Hinton is an expert in sexual predators. He

had to turn in his pastor father for preying on dozens of young girls, and he has spent his life trying to understand the mind of a predatory person. One of the talks he gives is about fruit. He cautions that narcissistic, sociopathic, and psychopathic people are extremely adept at manufacturing fake fruit. They appear righteous, but underneath they are wolves seeking to devour. Boz Tchividjian, the founder of Godly Response to Abuse in a Christian Environment (GRACE), advises that niceness is deceptive. It is not a character trait. Instead, it's learned behavior a predator uses to woo victims.

Perhaps the easiest way to discern a narcissistic friend is to watch them in public. Jesus gave us a perfect illustration:

> When you are invited to a wedding feast, don't sit in the seat of honor. What if someone who is more distinguished than you has also been invited? The host will come and say, "Give this person your seat." Then you will be embarrassed, and you will have to take whatever seat is left at the foot of the table! Instead, take the lowest place at the foot of the table. Then when your host sees you, he will come and say, "Friend, we have a better place for you!" Then you will be honored in front of all the other guests. For those who exalt themselves will be humbled, and those who humble themselves will be exalted" (Luke 14:8-11).

A narcissist thrives with honor and often seeks it out, demands it. He or she wants to be recognized in public. If you see this, be wary, because eventually that need for public recognition will morph into private requirements. In the context of relationship, a narcissistic person will demand constant heralding and unending (and unwarranted) praise in daily life. They constantly need ego stroking behind closed doors, and this can become exhausting.

And if you threaten to expose a narcissist, beware. Dr. Diane

Langberg shares an important truth: "When a narcissist is exposed, their horror is about the damage it will do *to them* to be accused and they believe that others are failing *them* by getting in the way of their ability to live out their specialness."[4] You will become a narcissist's sworn enemy. When you were "loved" as long as you existed to stroke their ego, you'll become hated when you don't.

Now What?

What should you do if you find yourself in a relationship with a narcissist? As mentioned before, find a way to separate in order to heal. Pray for your loved one. But don't engage for a period of time, perhaps forever. Much has been written about negotiating a relationship with narcissistic people, but it's not easy and takes a level of sophistication and prowess to navigate it well.

> The key, then, to interacting with someone you suspect is narcissistic is to break the vicious circle—to gently thwart their frantic efforts to control, distance, defend or blame in the relationship by sending the message that you're more than willing to connect with *them*, but not on these terms; to invite them into a version of intimacy where they can be loved and admired, warts and all—if they only allow the experience to happen.[5]

In other words, change the rules of the game. Instead of being vulnerable and letting the narcissist live on a stage of admiration, be cautious and dare the narcissistic friend to share vulnerably. Most often this cannot work. Why? Because if the narcissistic person has been acting this way his or her whole life, change is nearly impossible. Picture it like a needle going into the groove of an overplayed record. The more it's played, the deeper the groove, and the less likely the needle will skip out of that groove. Once self-serving behavior becomes a minute-by-minute, deeply entrenched habit, it's very difficult to change. Of course, through Christ anything is possible, which is why it's always wise to separate, heal, pray, forgive, and be ready in case your narcissistic friend comes to her senses. But I wouldn't be honest if I said that it's likely to happen. More often than not, a narcissist likes living that way and will not change.

AM I NARCISSIST NOLAN?

As I bulleted Narcissist Nolan's traits, I worried, *What if I am this kind of friend?* Because I've encountered quite a few narcissists in my life, I wondered if perhaps someone was writing a book about me and my self-centeredness. One thing I've learned about narcissists is that they are not self-aware. They do not and cannot examine themselves. So if you read the list and started worrying, chances are you're not a narcissist. The simple fact that you fretted about it is an indication that you have an examined life.

Another way to determine if you're this kind of friend is to see how Jesus defines it. He cautions all of us not to live haughty, prideful lives when he details the outcome of a Pharisee's and a tax collector's prayers.

> Then Jesus told this story to some who had great confidence in their own righteousness and scorned everyone else: "Two men went to the Temple to pray. One was a Pharisee, and the other was a despised tax collector. The Pharisee stood by himself and prayed this prayer: 'I thank you, God, that I am not like other people— cheaters, sinners, adulterers. I'm certainly not like that tax collector! I fast twice a week, and I give you a tenth of my income.' But the tax collector stood at a distance and dared not even lift his eyes to heaven as he prayed.

Instead, he beat his chest in sorrow, saying, 'O God, be merciful to me, for I am a sinner.' I tell you, this sinner, not the Pharisee, returned home justified before God. For those who exalt themselves will be humbled, and those who humble themselves will be exalted" (Luke 18:9-14).

Exalting oneself is a narcissist's full-time job. Weakness must be avoided. She must never admit to wrongdoing. Repentance is only for show (when a narcissistic person has been caught), or to demean someone else (because it's their fault), but never for personal contrition. So if you have apologized to a friend for hurting him, if you have wept before God admitting your sin, if you have examined your heart and asked for forgiveness, then chances are you're not a narcissist. It's not very likely that a person with narcissistic personality disorder will repent. But if you have repented and you can, consider yourself free.

The deeper question comes when you examine your life and see a pattern of chasing narcissists. This is my issue. As I mentioned in the beginning of this chapter, if you were raised by narcissistic people (whether by parents, grandparents, or even by interacting with narcissistic siblings), you tend to pursue them later in life. You do this because you have an unfinished story, and you long to see it completed. In my case, I subconsciously hoped that if I could get a narcissist to love me, I would finally prove I'm lovable to a narcissist, particularly my family of origin. It was a story I would never complete, simply because narcissistic people cannot truly love you. So instead of chasing narcissists, it's wiser to pursue healing—to let Jesus finish your broken love story with his love. We'll talk about how to do this in the latter chapters.

But not all of you reading this book have my unique experience. Sometimes narcissistic people are simply attractive, life-of-the-party folks we long to be associated with. We want to be in the popular crowd, and sometimes narcissists stand out attractively within those groups. I know I've chased after friends who fit this mold simply because they exuded confidence, fun, and liveliness. The frustrating truth is that narcissistic people are incredibly attractive in the short term. They perform well in short spurts. And those spurts attract us.

We will always have Narcissist Nolans in this world. They tend to thrive, particularly when their narcissism doesn't catch up with them. But we can be wise about how we choose to deal with them. And we don't have to be a game piece in their self-serving game. Like Tyler, we can uncover these Quick Changers and simply stop making transactions for them. And as we separate, we can always pray, process, and forgive.

2

Unreliable Uma

"A Lying Tongue"

cried on the phone with my new friend. Something she also faced
had come to bite me, so I felt safe sharing my heartache. She would
understand since she had walked my path before. Besides, she'd
been tasked with leading us as we faced a new ministry experience.

"Well, um, I don't really know what to say," she said.

I restated the difficult situation, this time emphasizing my own
heartache and how it intersected hers.

She backpedaled, seemingly shocked at my sadness. Repulsed
by it, actually. She mumbled something about choosing to be
strong and then hung up. I should have known then not to entrust
my heart to her, but I gave it the old college try and continued
(unwisely) to pursue her. Eventually, my neediness in a very difficult situation turned her against me, and she met my sadness with
surliness. And then she mocked me.

Which was when I stopped pursuing her. Our friendship only
worked if I had no needs. And in the aftermath of it all, I realized,
too, that my own authentic sharing rocked her. She'd spent a lifetime playacting the perfect Christian wife and life, never mining

what she really felt. So when crazy me with all my communication and realness met her, our tenuous friendship inevitably failed. We were unequally yoked, but not in the way you might think.

She wanted only friends who would hang out with her, praise her, and have few needs. As long as that dynamic persisted, she engaged in the friendship. But the moment a real need arose, she bailed.

Have you experienced this kind of unreliable friend? This friend loves you when you're fine, when you have no needs or flaws. But throw in a messy situation like death of a loved one or divorce of a spouse, and this friend suddenly becomes busy with another "easier" friend. When she leaves, she blames you for your problems, making you feel small and overly needy. Living day in and day out with friends like this can be exhausting; they drain your soul because you realize you cannot truly be yourself, and you are only loved for your happy, put-together self.

As a novelist, I'm well aware of what's called the unreliable narrator. That's the person who tells the story, and if the storyteller is unreliable, the reader cannot trust what they say. This makes for great mysteries, but it is entirely unhelpful in life. Unreliable narrators knowingly hold important details back. They tell only their side of the story, skewing truth to suit their own me-centered narrative. This is a perfect picture of a friend who's unreliable. They typically process their explanations and excuses to benefit themselves, and they don't seem to hold a moral compass to tell the truth, particularly when it makes them look bad.

TRAITS

Unreliable Uma behaves this way:

- When you express a clear need, your friend does not respond or creates excuses to not engage.

- She changes the subject when you begin to emote about a current painful situation.

- She throws Christian clichés your way, peppered with ripped-out-of-context Bible verses in hopes that placing that spiritual Band-Aid on you will quiet your pain.

- Your gut tells you something's wrong, or you have a vague feeling of being used after each interaction.

- Conversely, other friends have told you that you're in a one-sided, fair-weather friendship. (Sometimes we can't see clearly, and we need the discernment of other good friends to perceive what's really going on.)

- Her sacrifice is miniscule, while yours (in the relationship) feels exhausting.

- You hear from mutual friends that she is tired of your complaining.

- She makes fun of you for having pain in the first place, telling you to buck up and get over it.

- She blames you for your pain.

- She does not celebrate your accomplishments, and you get the impression that she's jealous and angry when you succeed.

- She tells you to get over your pain, to move on.

- She doesn't seem to want you to grow in your relationship with Christ, be your best self, or improve your habits.

- She seems gleeful when you fail.

- She never apologizes for obvious violations in the relationship, but she demands that you constantly say you're sorry.

- The friendship isn't reciprocal.

- She breaks engagements consistently and constantly.

- You can't be yourself around her because she doesn't really accept who you really are.

- She keeps you in her back pocket, but constantly pursues other exciting relationships.

- Similarly, she easily points out your faults, while changing the subject if you return the favor.

- The friendship feels more complicated than easy and joyful.

- She sulks when she doesn't get her way.

- The friendship feels more like an obligatory transaction rather than a convivial exchange. You're always aware when you "owe" her something. She keeps track of everything she's done and sometimes uses language like, "You owe me."

- She is a poor listener, but demands that you be a great one.

- She shares your intimate details as gossip with others, maligning your neediness.

- Instead of empathizing with your plight, she shares that her pain is worse and you should be grateful you're not experiencing what she has.

- She has mastered the put-down (of you), but expects you to elevate her when she's sad.

- She berates you for sharing your need, inferring you're ungrateful or ungodly.

- You perceive or notice that she doesn't have your back.

- She doesn't pursue you, ask questions of you, or seem interested in your current plight.

- You're never entirely sure if she's telling you the truth.

- You feel used after you connect with her.

- She "ghosts" you when you're in need. (Won't take calls, stops following you on social media with no explanation, etc.)

- She opts to go out with her "fun friends" when you're at your lowest—and she may lie about her availability so she can have fun with them.

- She agrees to meet, but then doesn't show up, or at the last minute sends you a text full of excuses.

- She looks visibly drained when you ask for a small favor.

- She is very "there" for you if it suits her needs or she wants something from you.

- She offers general advice about your situation, preferring to placate you with vague platitudes.

- She never asks you about yourself. You always have to volunteer information about your life. However, she often goes on long soliloquys about her issues.

- She calls you only when no one else is available. You're her last call.

- She praises herself and the way she does things (including how she processes pain), and puts you down for the way you navigate a difficult time.

INTERACTIONS WITH UNRELIABLE UMA

Selma's elementary school friend became an Unreliable Uma. "My dad took his life three years ago, and, like the suicide of my late spouse, it again rocked my being. My friend from elementary school, someone I thought I could be open to and free to grieve openly with, ran as fast as she could when I no longer smiled for a while or could muster joy. All the friendship spaces we have had for so many years would not face the darkness of suicide loss. I did not choose this. She did. It breaks my heart." Note how long Selma and her friend had cultivated a friendship: years. And in one painful instance, everything fell.

Jared shares about several Unreliable Umas from his own church. "In college I went to a church that preached a lot about loving your neighbor and community. Small groups were supposed to solve any of your problems. One night, due to some complicated college shenanigans, I was locked out of my apartment and had to wait till the next morning to get in. I figured this wouldn't be a big problem; I just had to call up one of my many so-called friends to crash on their couch. It was 8:00 p.m.—which was basically noon in college time. But every friend I called either didn't answer, or couldn't help, or didn't know of any way to help. After a half dozen calls or so, I ended up walking to a hotel and paying fifty bucks for a night. But in my college days I had let people crash at my place several times, and it was no problem or inconvenience," Jared writes.

This became the final straw as he realized how unchristian his group of friends from church was. "This was incredible because the number-one stereotype of the folks from this church was that they were overly nice. I'm not exactly a needy person. I once walked to church when my car was broken because I just didn't think to ask someone for a ride. What I mean is I don't often ask for help for things, but the one time I actually needed help, all my friends weren't there. Afterward I was able to get a ride to go get my keys back. But I asked one of my school friends, not my church friends. First person I called helped me out."

Jane dealt with an unreliable and underhanded coworker. "Ellie and I worked together for several years in ministry," she said. "She was one of my closest confidants when I was going through a difficult time. I really treasured her as a friend. One day I thought about looking for another job. I had previously used the professional services of her best friend, Rebekah. Rebekah remarked that I was really good about navigating the complicated processes [involved in her company] and would love to hire me one day if I ever thought about leaving my current job. I decided to reach out to Rebekah privately. I explained to her that I was interested in a position at her agency, if one was available, and asked that she please keep my desire confidential. Rebekah responded almost immediately and said that there weren't any current openings, but if one became available, that I would be the first person she would call."

Jane continued, "A few days later Ellie asked me to go to lunch with her." In that conversation, Ellie told Jane that Rebekah *had* disclosed Jane's desire to leave her current position. So Ellie asked Jane if she, instead, wanted a different position within the ministry—to keep her there so she wouldn't pursue outside employment with Rebekah. Jane said yes, then continued. "For about a month or so, she would check in with me periodically to see if I was still interested in the different ministry position, but nothing was really materializing in the form of a new position in her department." One day Ellie told Jane that she decided to leave her current ministry position and took the position with Rebekah instead. Jane said, "I went home that evening and I got mad. It took me a few hours, but I realized what Ellie did. She received confidential information from her friend Rebekah, then seized the opportunity to get a job at the agency—the job I wanted! And she strung me along for a month by telling me that she would work on finding me a new position in her department."

Anna has felt the sting of indifference in her role as a pastor's wife. "I feel this keenly as a pastor's wife, and I know I'm not alone. We spend our lives being there for people in all of their ups and downs (quite a roller coaster for the pastor's family, considering how many people are often under our care). While we deeply love caring for people, it's true that many friends are nowhere to be found when we ourselves suffer. I think this is pretty common in ministry...especially in places where people are so caught up in the rat race that they have little time for genuine, deep relationships. Grab-n-go is how this feels when it happens in friendship. It's a fast-food relationship, with no time or desire to linger at the table and savor."

Grace walked through a dark time when her ministry leader (and boss) suddenly died. She writes, "I have a group of five friends that group-text daily. We talk about everything from the new Starbucks latte flavors, to prayers for our kids and marriages, to confession of sin...everything is talked about. We have been friends for ten years. We have traveled together for weddings and new babies. But in this season of grief and leading while grieving, where I'm fully spent daily, my friends haven't been there. Sure, I can text a prayer request, but they simply aren't showing up. I don't think they understand what it feels like to experience significant grief. The kind that doesn't go away and hurts deeply." Grace has had trouble sharing her need for them to just be present and spend time with her. She writes, "It all kind of climaxed the other day because one of the five had a stomach bug and another friend went over to clean her house and watch her kids. I've been sick five times since the pastor died, and they haven't visited once. They don't even ask me about it. Again, I don't think they understand. But it has left me feeling very insecure in a season of depletion. God has been good, as he always is. So, are they unreliable? My husband thinks so! I hope that they just don't understand."

Mara has experienced a similar loss. "I had friends who were friends when they needed something from me or I didn't have any needs. If I could serve them, be there for them at any time, do exactly what they wanted, they were happy to be my friends. Now I am walking through a very deep valley with my husband's health and caring for my aging in-laws, and they are gone like the wind." Even so, Mara has found hope. "The wonderful thing is this: God has provided true friends and family who are walking our journey with us. In the trenches. In the tears. In the turmoil. They continually offer practical help, encouraging words, Scripture to remind us of our hope, and more. Sometimes it takes the valley to see who are the friends who stick closer than a brother. And in the long run, those are the friends I want in my life."

WHAT THE BIBLE SAYS

What Mara expresses is beautiful, and she hints at the silver lining of these kinds of friends who abandon you in your need: You learn who your real friends are. And in that learning, you find your resilience, though finding it can bring pain.

Job faced this realization when he spoke to his "comforters," friends who instead of empathizing blamed Job for his pain. He wrote eloquently about unreliable friends: "My brothers, you have proved as unreliable as a seasonal brook that overflows its banks in the spring when it is swollen with ice and melting snow. But when the hot weather arrives, the water disappears. The brook vanishes in the heat" (Job 6:15-17). In other words, when things got dicey for Job, when he needed his friends the most, they abandoned him.

Sometimes you're so involved in a friendship that you cannot see clearly what is going on. You may need to have some brave conversations with others outside the relationship to truly discern how you're being treated. We tend to love what we know. We love unchange. We sometimes worship the status quo, preferring it to rocking the boat of a so-so friendship. Thankfully, friends who really love you will point out when you're walking in painful territory.

I'm reminded of one particular friend (I'll call her Carol) who constantly put me down. I didn't realize it at the time, but she was often like this: "One should be kind to a fainting friend, but you accuse me without any fear of the Almighty" (Job 6:14). Instead of helping me when I fainted, she blamed me for passing out. It wasn't until two of my best friends sat me down and reflected back what Carol was doing that my eyes were opened. What confounded it all was the longevity of the relationship. We had started out very well, but over several years, our interaction deteriorated. All that history kept me blind to the current reality, and it wasn't until I started sharing my unease that my friends helped open my eyes.

"She's a bully," one of them told me.

Initially, I balked and pushed back. But as I began to see the situation through the eyes of two women who loved me well, I knew they were right. I had to make a very painful choice to address the issues. Unfortunately, when I brought up Carol's behavior to her, she bullied me all the more, and our friendship did not survive. While I have grieved (and continue to grieve) this friendship, I remember the distinct feeling of peace I felt when I was no longer her friend. It felt like I'd exhaled several years of pain and breathed in freedom.

The psalmist got right to the point when he wrote, "I will not allow deceivers to serve in my house, and liars will not stay in my presence" (Psalm 101:7). While it's not necessary to completely sever a relationship with Unreliable Uma (as I believe is the case for narcissistic and predatory friends), you do have a choice in how you interact with her. If her unreliability and deception grow worse, and you constantly feel maligned or pushed away (like you're an eye-rolling inconvenience), then you get to choose to set up boundaries. You don't have to allow folks like this to control your life. If you stop adding fuel to the one-sided friendship fire, you'll realize quickly how much of your effort kept it alive. In other words, without your spark, the friendship flame flickers out.

Perhaps part of our problem with these types of unreliable friends is our tenacious clinging to any and all friends. When I became a Christian as a teenager, I gathered a false belief to myself that my Christian friends would be my forever friends. Surely, since we both loved Jesus and followed him, we would always be in each other's lives. No one would hurt the other—because of Jesus! It didn't take long for that theory of mine to be tested by reality.

I moved away, naively thinking my friends back "home" would always want to be in my life. Although none of us broke up with one another, the move did that for us. It's simply hard to be super close when you live super far away. Over the years I've experienced several soft breakups caused by moving from place to place. Even though I'm a clinger, and I try to make every friendship endure the lengthy contours of life, I've finally made peace with the fact that things change. People change. Locations change us. Some friends God brings into our lives are for a sweet season, and then it's time to move on.

Perhaps this friend who prefers your smile to your frown is a seasonal friend—one to let go of. Or maybe, through the foothills of time, God will bring redemption to a once one-sided friendship. Learning to forgive that friend and leaving room for God to work may just usher in future reconciliation.

Most of the traits mentioned above had to do with a friend not wanting to engage with your pain, but the opposite is also true. Some unreliable friends enjoy your mess, almost to the point of glee, but they cannot be happy for you. They do not adhere to the first part of Paul's admonition: "Be happy with those who are happy, and weep with those who weep" (Romans 12:15). Weeping? Yes. Happy for you? No. My friend Sandi has told me that the true mark of a friendship (and she is really good at this) is that your friend can rejoice with your success. This is a hallmark of his or her maturity and security.

Which leads us to this: Some people are simply not mature. They may need a hall pass from you during this season of immaturity, as you gently lead and guide them toward wisdom. But if they continue to live foolishly, it may be time to distance yourself. I'm indebted to the book of Proverbs, chock full of wisdom about how we should interact with foolish people (or "fools," as the author calls them). Proverbs 18:2 reminds us of one important trait of foolish people: They are unable to listen. "Fools have no interest in understanding; they only want to air their own opinions."

Unreliable Uma is more interested in being listened to than actively listening. She doesn't ask clarifying (and life-giving questions) to better understand your heart. Her goal is to force you to understand every nuance of hers while living in indifference toward even the superficial aspect of yours.

One of the disciplines I've pursued when I'm walking through relational difficulty is to read and reread Proverbs. It's brimming with insight. Consider this:

> Let the wise listen to these proverbs and become even wiser. Let those with understanding receive guidance by exploring the meaning in these proverbs and parables, the words of the wise and their riddles. Fear of the Lord is the foundation of true knowledge, but fools despise wisdom and discipline (Proverbs 1:5-7).

Solomon's advice is twofold: Fear God first, and then embrace wisdom and discipline. Fearing God (more than you fear an Unreliable Uma's opinion of you) helps keep you safe. It reminds you that his ways, his love, his relationship with you will be the only thing that truly fills you up. If she is high on unreliability, God is the epitome of true faithfulness—the friend who will never leave or forsake you. Because he is *for* you, he will empower you, even when your heart breaks when someone seems against you. This passage also offers an important clue about a fool: He or she simply will not seek after wisdom, nor will he live a life of discipline.

The other thing that tends to happen with Unreliable Uma is that she continues to be unreliable. It's one thing if she has flaked on you a few times during a particularly stressful period of life. (We all have friends like that, and we all are friends like that. Life presses in!) But if she continues to display a pattern of unreliability to the point that you've stopped believing her, and she continually disappoints even your smallest expectations, you may need to reassess the relationship. Proverbs 26:11 reminds us of this graphic truth: "As a dog returns to its vomit, so a fool repeats his foolishness." The truth? You don't have to bear witness to your unreliable friend's repetitious behavior.

The best way to work through this uncomfortable situation is to heed Jesus's instructions in Matthew 18:15-17:

> If another believer sins against you, go privately and point out the offense. If the other person listens and confesses it, you have won that person back. But if you are unsuccessful, take one or two others with you and go back again, so that everything you say may be confirmed by two or three witnesses. If the person still refuses to listen, take your case to the church. Then if he or she won't accept the church's decision, treat that person as a pagan or a corrupt tax collector.

While unreliability isn't necessarily the kind of sin you'd drag out in front of the church, Jesus's pattern here is important. First, go to your friend. Tell him or her what you're feeling, how lately they've seemed unreliable. Talk it out. Ask questions. Assume positive intent. By doing this, you may end up salvaging the relationship. What tends to happen in friendships like this, though, is that we get exasperated and reverse Jesus's instructions. We go to everyone else (taking our case to the church), complaining about Unreliable Uma. Instead of kindly confronting, we blare her "sins" to others. Gossip ensures that reconciliation won't happen. So go to her first, with kindness and truth, and see how she responds.

If you want to enhance your discernment of Unreliable Uma and other deadly friendships, read Proverbs 12:15-25:

> Fools think their own way is right, but the wise listen to others.
>
> A fool is quick-tempered, but a wise person stays calm when insulted.
>
> An honest witness tells the truth; a false witness tells lies.
>
> Some people make cutting remarks, but the words of the wise bring healing.
>
> Truthful words stand the test of time, but lies are soon exposed.
>
> Deceit fills hearts that are plotting evil; joy fills hearts that are planning peace!
>
> No harm comes to the godly, but the wicked have their fill of trouble.
>
> The Lord detests lying lips, but he delights in those who tell the truth.
>
> The wise don't make a show of their knowledge, but fools broadcast their foolishness.

Work hard and become a leader; be lazy and become a slave.

Worry weighs a person down; an encouraging word cheers a person up.

Based on these verses, the Lord is reminding us to be wary of people who don't listen, get mad quickly, lie, cut people down, plot evil (we'll look at this more in depth in chapter 4, Conman Connor), invite trouble, and broadcast their foolish antics. If you have a friend, family member, or spouse who fits a majority of these traits, it may be time to reevaluate to whom you entrust your heart. Proverbs 25:19 cautions, "Putting confidence in an unreliable person in times of trouble is like chewing with a broken tooth or walking on a lame foot."

As I write this, I'm about to see a dentist about a broken tooth. I can assure you that chewing on one is no fun. It never improves with time. Instead, it screams to be fixed. Similarly, we cannot ignore foolish behavior forever, hoping it will go away. Instead, we must address it.

The way in which we bring up our concerns is also detailed in the Proverbs 12 passage above. The author encourages us to first become a person who listens. Instead of jumping to conclusions, we ask clarifying questions.

In Joshua 22, we see a perfectly sad picture of a people who jumped to negative conclusions. After the nation of Israel began settling in the land of Canaan on the western side of the Jordan River, a few tribes settled on the eastern side and built an altar there. This caused the western tribes to jump to conclusions, thinking Reuben, Gad, and the half tribe of Manasseh were building their own altar, seemingly establishing their own nation apart from the whole—an act of war.

Thankfully, they had a perfectly viable explanation for their actions:

The truth is, we have built this altar because we fear that in the future your descendants will say to ours, "What right do you have to worship the Lord, the God of Israel? The Lord has placed the Jordan River as a barrier between our people and you people of Reuben and Gad. You have no claim to the Lord." So your descendants may prevent our descendants from worshiping the Lord. So we decided to build the altar, not for burnt offerings or sacrifices, but as a memorial" (Joshua 22:24-27).

In the light of sensible conversation and listening, war was averted. It's the same for us. When we listen and ask questions, we may find out that our staunchly held view of our friend's actions may be completely off the mark.

In this exchange with the Israelites, the eastern tribes also demonstrated staying calm when insulted. So many conflicts in relationships, whether with an unreliable friend or another type of relationship, could be solved by one of us choosing *not* to react angrily. Taking a deep breath after being insulted prevents the kinds of outbursts that sever relationships.

The Proverbs 12 passage also underscores the importance of telling the truth. Paul reminds us of the manner in which we share that truth: "We will speak the truth in love, growing in every way more and more like Christ, who is the head of his body, the church" (Ephesians 4:15). Always, always, we season our words with love, expecting the best of the person.

I once met a woman who loved to spew truth. When I talked to her about the way she hurt people with her words, she said, "I'm just being authentic." She spoke as if authenticity was the highest value one could have. I had to remind her that we're still to love others. It may be "real" to holler whatever comes to our mind, but as we submit to the Spirit, he will empower us to have self-control with the manner in which we share.

We must all keep in mind Paul's instructions about love when we speak truth to Unreliable Uma:

> Love is patient and kind. Love is not jealous or boastful or proud or rude. It does not demand its own way. It is not irritable, and it keeps no record of being wronged. It does not rejoice about injustice but rejoices whenever the truth wins out. Love never gives up, never loses faith, is always hopeful, and endures through every circumstance (1 Corinthians 13:4-7).

Our words, according to Proverbs 12, must usher in healing, not devastation—peace, not discord. We don't speak truth to reveal our awesome knowledge, but to bring understanding and the possibility of reconciliation. And above all, we are to be people of encouragement. When bringing up your feelings, first remind yourself why you pursued Unreliable Uma in the first place. Highlight her strengths; thank her for how she's been in the past.

These are never easy conversations, but there does exist a good possibility that you can grow in your understanding of Unreliable Uma if you dare to pursue her this way, with a listening heart and a desire for change in the relationship. However, Unreliable Uma may not respond well to your overtures. All you can do is your part. Paul asserts, "Do all that you can to live in peace with everyone" (Romans 12:18). Once you've said your piece (and peace!), you can rest in knowing you tried. Also remember that reconciliation doesn't always happen. And it seldom happens in your timing.

I had an Unreliable Uma in my life whom I confronted (gently) because she was in a very difficult place. She heard what I said, but I know she was hurt. Several years went by where we had zero contact.

Later, she called me. When I saw her number, I got a stomachache. But I answered anyway. Turned out, she took my words to heart, had an amazing encounter with Jesus, and wanted to reconcile. I count her today as one of my most faithful, encouraging friends.

The Unreliable Uma mentioned at the beginning of this chapter is still estranged from me. There was no "breakup" per se. Time, moving, and distance caused the separation. And I have no unction to pursue her across the miles. I'm actually grateful she's not in my life.

All that to say, some of these friends may return to you better than before. Others may desert you. And some may simply fade away with the seasons of life.

AM I UNRELIABLE UMA?

I believe we all are Unreliable Uma at different parts of our lives. Who of us hasn't dropped the ball for a friend who needed us? Who hasn't flaked on an invitation? The question we must ask ourselves is whether our unreliability is a pattern in our lives. To find that out, look to the times in your life when no one is watching. Are you faithful then? Jesus reminds us, "If you are faithful in little things, you will be faithful in large ones. But if you are dishonest in little things, you won't be honest with greater responsibilities" (Luke 16:10). How we are when no one is looking is truly who we are. And when we are unfaithful in small, unnoticed things, we tend to be unfaithful friends, particularly when our friends need us the most.

Jesus also reminds us to be frank, to mean what we say and say what we mean. He said, "Just say a simple, 'Yes, I will,' or 'No, I won't.' Anything beyond this is from the evil one" (Matthew 5:37). If you cancel on a friend using an excuse (instead of the truth), you'll be training yourself to be unreliable. Let your words mean what they say. Don't fear people so much that you have to make up stories and excuses to say no.

That being said, saying no is a powerful tool. It helps your friends know your limits and boundaries. It also helps you understand who your reliable friends are. Reliable friends love your no as much as they love your yes. They understand you are an autonomous person, loved by Jesus, who gets to say what you do and don't want. You may not always make your friends happy by saying no, but to the degree in which a friend pushes against your no is the possible degree they may become a problematic relationship in the future.

The best way to find out if you are Unreliable Uma is to ask six friends whether they think you're reliable—three of your closest friends as well as three acquaintances. This isn't easy to do, but will provide excellent intel for your own sanctification journey.

We all have unreliable friends in our lives, and we have all been unreliable. As sinners saved by grace, we fall and stumble many times, but God is good and will empower us to become more and more faithful. He embodies reliability, and he loves to help us become faithful friends to others.

3

PREDATOR PAIGE

"Hands That Kill the Innocent"

Our last conversation still reverberates through me. The harsh words. The agonizing silences where I felt the pulse in my throat. The shaky feeling one gets when biting sentences are perfectly spewed, and they are meant to harm you in your weakest spots. All my buttons were pushed. Stabbed, actually.

In the whirlwind of our final conversation, flashbacks taunted me. How she bullied me into compliance. When she tried to force me to do something against my conscience so she would look better. How I'd uncovered the way she exploited others, robbing them of resources and time. The sick feeling I got whenever I hung up the phone.

Yet in the midst of that tornado, I also recalled the beauty: the long conversations of empathy, the mutual cheerleading, and the casual times shared over a meal.

Why was it so hard to come to grips with the fact that I had, once again, befriended a predatory person? Precisely because they are predators parading around in friends' clothing. They're adept, highly skilled psychopathic or sociopathic people who have perfected their technique. They woo. They appear philanthropic. They sometimes possess the characteristics you lack but need in a friend. They're popular, charming, the life of the party. They have the ability to cast a spell on you without you realizing it.

I fell under that spell, only to regret it years later while my phone felt hot to my ears and her words sliced through me.

I hung up, stood, and walked to my office. I put my face in my hands and whelped out a guttural cry. The rawness of it all overcame me. The tension I sensed during the call, how my shoulders nearly reached my ears as I listened. Finally, I released nearly a decade of tears.

"It's over. It's over," I said over and over again.

The friendship was *over*.

The ending came swift and final, ending in a wail, not a whimper.

I still dream of my friend, still think to call her, only to remind myself of the hazards of doing so. Although I've unfollowed her on social media, from time to time she pops up, and I hurt all over again. I backpedal. I question. I reminisce about the good times, questioning myself again as to why it had to end. I fret about what she says about me now that we're no longer friends. Will she capitalize on my vulnerability? Share my secrets? Bad-mouth me? Or will she find another person to victimize?

Before you paint me in that victim light, I am well aware of my own contribution to the friendship's demise. Ours was a mutual breakup. But even realizing that blame lived on both sides didn't mean the whole fiasco didn't injure us both. In the aftermath of that phone call, we were both broken. I couldn't call her for consolation. And she couldn't call me either. We would process our grief with other friends, no longer integral parts of each other's lives. Our shared history, seemingly a living document between us, is now shredded, never to be reassembled in some sort of reunification collage.

Even so, in blessed retrospect, I'm utterly grateful she's not my friend anymore.

It's an agonizing grief, losing a predatory friend—particularly when that friendship ends in a breakup. But even harder is discovering why I pursued Predator Paige in the first place. As I look back on some of my broken friendships, I piece together uncomfortable truths. I tend to pursue people who are not good for me, and I hang on far too long, risking deeper injury. So often I am trying to complete an untethered part of my own story—usually from childhood. I pursue the same kind of people who harmed me in an unconscious desire to complete an incomplete story.

One day I saw the "twin" of one of my first predatory friends in the church. Her voice sounded just like hers. Her face looked the same too. As did her demeanor with her kids. In one moment, I felt sickness rise up in my throat. I held my stomach. I thanked God it wasn't her, but my physical reaction reminded me of the past pain. I'd heard enough of her cruel words to curdle my soul—times when she yelled at me, backed me into a corner (literally), and demeaned me in front of my children. The words still spoil inside me today, shaking my resolve. Jealous words. Evil words. Lies. Backbiting. Sneers. Jeers. Haughty, proud words. Words meant to impale. Words said with a painted-on smile but meant with malice.

Why did seeing her twin trigger me, flashing memories before me like a cruel comic strip? Mainly because encountering a predator often ushers in symptoms of PTSD. And if that relationship is long term, their lingering effects continue to this day, haunting us at unusual times.

As I've mentioned before, upbringing has something to do with entangling ourselves in, then living in the aftermath of Predator Paige's rampages. Growing up, I was not cherished, not wanted, an imposition, always at fault. All these factors swirled their way like a toxic stew into my fragile ego. I pursued everyone—even people who were decidedly bad for me—hoping I could reverse the truth of my perceived unworthiness. I could win over a predator! I could prove my ability to overcome even the gravest obstacles lurking in a predator's heart.

Except that predatory people seldom use caution when they hurt others. They say awful things. They physically abuse you. Some sexually attack you. And if you're broken from the past, you might believe you deserve every foul word, every trampling on, or every cruel dismissal.

And oddly, there's a strange comfort in living with a predator. It's your normal, what you expect, what you deserve. It feels right. It may be awful, but it resembles the sameness of your past situation, so in a twisted way, it's comforting, this relationship. You may naively believe that if you could just perform better, you could magically change someone's opinion from an angry stench to joyful flowers.

Thinking about this particular predatory friend and watching her life unfold, I've learned the sad truth that people usually don't change. If they make their livelihood out of belittling others, there's a strange intoxication in it. They get drunk off their feelings of power over folks. They love the upper hand. They may even want to change, but it's hard going. Unless Jesus swoops in (and they welcome his swooping) and showers grace upon grace, there is little hope for lasting change.

I can't swoop in. I've tried. Only Jesus can do heart surgery like that.

The intoxicating power predators wield over us cannot be underestimated. I recall one day where I'd been tempted to send flowers to one, hoping to make her like me. I wrestled over the decision. I wanted to send those flowers as much as I wanted Lindt Dark Chocolate with Lime Filling. Eventually, I decided not to. Because sending the flowers to a predator would be another invitation to cruelty. And my soul has had enough of that.

The difficult truth is this: If we have been victimized in the past, we are more susceptible to falling prey to a predator in the present.

We not only have blinders to predatory behavior or signs, but we seem to have a sign etched in our soul that welcomes predators.

I wrote about the phenomenon in my book about sexual abuse, *Not Marked: Finding Hope and Healing after Sexual Abuse*. It's been one of the largest points of healing in my life to finally let go of that mark, but it hasn't been easy. I assumed that when the lion's share of my healing happened in my early twenties, I'd be blessedly unmarked to predators, and I could go on my Mary way. This overconfidence kept me blind to several predatory folks, both men and women, who crept into my life. Because my discernment was compromised in this area, I let those folks in and paid the price later. I'm wiser now, but still vulnerable. I must maintain vigilance.

As I've mentioned earlier, when I'm preyed upon, I don't fight or flee; I freeze. When a Christian writing industry professional placed his hand on my leg during what I thought was a professional meeting, I didn't slap him (I should have). Instead I froze, which then gave him the message that this type of behavior was okay. I had to spend a lot of time and energy protecting myself from him because of this.

One wouldn't expect to be inappropriately touched by a Christian professional, right? But that's what makes predators all the more cunning. They often masquerade as angels of light in bright and shiny ministry places. They're typically brilliant at wordplay, gaslighting, and manipulation. In short, they're not who you expect them to be.

So who is Predator Paige? How can you spot her?

TRAITS

Predator Paige behaves this way:

- She seems too perfect. She seemingly has everything together.
- She is admirable, the kind of person you'd want to emulate.

- She is a master of deceit.

- She hides her sociopathic tendencies by creating admirable facades that fit nicely into each situation.

- She tends to distract you easily from her faults, making others out to be the reason she even has tiny faults (it's all someone else's fault).

- She easily morphs into what you admire.

- She seems to enjoy shaming you into submission.

- Her daily currency is deceit. She cannot tell the truth or discern it.

- Many of the predatory adults I have known (not all, but a sizable amount) are not on social media. Predator Paige protects her privacy like crazy.

- She tends to completely reinvent herself every few years with brand-new friends whom she can display her "perfection" to. This is also true of Conman Connor, who initially charms everyone, then exploits all his relationships, and then moves away or reinvents himself somewhere else. In light of this, be cautious of a charismatic newcomer to your group of friends.

- She is entitled. She believes everything is owed to her, and she is entitled to special treatment. She has the corner on the market of wisdom, power, and prestige, and therefore seeks to be served instead of serving others.

- Others exist to serve her needs. She has the impugnable right to do whatever she wants, often without any pushback.

- Often Predator Paige moves so stealthily between

victims (and so frightens or shames them) that she seemingly gets away with multiple offenses throughout her life span. Not only entitled, she's Teflon. Nothing sticks—which furthers her grandiosity.

- She is a master at exploitation. She knows your weaknesses and blind spots (though oblivious to her own). She will press for very deep, intimate knowledge of your life (often right away when you first meet her) in order to use that sensitive information against you later. In light of knowing your triggers, she will push your buttons and manipulate you into doing whatever it is she wants you to do.

- She tends to be moody toward you. Praising you incessantly one day, to completely ignoring and ghosting you the next. This keeps you off kilter, never knowing when your friend will be kind or simply abandon you. It's feast or famine.

- Like Narcissist Ned, Predator Paige has a hard time telling the actual truth. She simply manufactures her own, with a lengthy narrative that she overplays, wearing you down until you believe the concocted stories as truth.

- Her abuse is not limited to physical abuse (although that is a possibility, as well as sexual abuse). Some of her most cunning abuse comes in the form of emotional abuse where she systematically dismantles the best parts of you, simply with words.

- She is unfaithful, and may cheat on you to keep you close or provoke jealousy.

- After the initial honeymoon phase, she uses intimidation,

ridicule, and shame with abandon. She knows your trigger points and pushes them, seemingly with glee. She uses veiled (and not-so-veiled) sarcasm and sadistic language to keep you from asserting yourself. She seems to demean often, but with a smile on her face—all in good fun.

- She gaslights. She says things one day and denies she said them the next. She makes promises, and when she doesn't keep them, she blames you for remembering those promises wrongly or making them up entirely. This kind of sophisticated manipulation is hard to discern, particularly for those who want to be kindhearted and give Predator Paige the benefit of the doubt. "Maybe I did hear that wrong," you might say to yourself.

- She rules by fear, not by grace. In her presence you will feel small and needy, and in some ways, you will need her in your life to feel okay about yourself. (She's made you believe you're incomplete without her.) Predator Paige longs for this kind of one-sided, needy dependence. She thrives when you're the messed-up one, and she is your savior.

- She will delight in making you violate your conscience. And she will continue to ask you to step farther and farther away from what you know is the right thing to do.

- She feigns intimacy. Predators are chameleons. She understands that intimacy is important, so she pretends to be whatever it is you need from her. She does this to gain your trust. But her heart is not in it. Instead, she playacts her way toward false intimacy. She demands your unswerving allegiance, but she will never truly share her heart. This keeps you confused and off balance.

- She must have control. Predators thrive in one situation: when they have control over another person. If a victim tries to assert his or her rights, Predator Paige will demean, cajole, threaten, harm, or even pretend to be hurt in order to maintain control. She must have complete autonomy over your decisions, thoughts, actions, and interactions with others.

- She will often isolate you from others who would help you discern the toxicity of the relationship, separating you from family and close friends who could offer a way of escape. This is why when a victim begins to assert his or her rights, sparks fly. Huge fights erupt when you begin to stand up. At this point you will either be further slammed into submission, or you will need to flee. (If that's you, go to a safe place. And then pursue counseling and health. You chose to be with this person for various reasons, and it's important you learn why you're attracted to predators. Get healthy before you approach a new relationship, or you might end up with another predator.)

- She sometimes suffers from low self-worth. It seems counterintuitive. You would think predatory people didn't ever need to think about self-worth since they gain power from hurting or controlling others. But some do so because they're deeply ashamed of themselves. Most bullies bully others because they are deeply unhappy. They're usually compensating for some sort of early childhood wound. Instead of grieving their past in a healthy way, they are making others pay for their sadness.

- Like a narcissist, she cannot empathize. While she may appear to empathize (she's learned how so she can blend in with normal, empathetic society), she absolutely cannot empathize with others. She is so consumed with herself and has no concept of other people's pain, boundaries, or even autonomy. She's the kind of person who will listen and appear to hear your molehill of hurt, but then will quickly change the subject to her own mountain of pain.

- She either loves or hates. There is no neutral ground. Predatory people can quickly demonize anyone who is against them. Or they overly fawn over someone they "love" with flattery that seems over the top. A loved one can quickly morph (in an instant) from a companion to an absolute enemy. I've experienced this several times, where one moment I was over-the-top loved and praised, then suddenly became the most evil, awful enemy known to man—from Jesus-like to satanic. Predator Paige doesn't keep silent about her enemies, either. She will tell her new victims all about the evil people in her past in order to gain your empathy (and also subtly warn you to *never* do that to her). If someone constantly talks about evil people or the evil they do, run away. Because someday she will say those very things about you. The intensity of her love today is only matched by the virulent hatred she holds for you tomorrow.

- She easily finds fault—but not in herself. Predator Paige blames everyone else for her issues or where she is in life. She is obsessive about other people's sin, but cannot ever see her own. And if you bring up her sin, wait for an explosion and expect to be blamed. She's masterful at blaming the blamers.

- She is likable and often popular. This one is the hardest

trait to swallow. When we think of predatory people, we think of creeps in white vans trolling neighborhoods for kids to harm. But Predator Paige is actually quite normal on the outside. She knows how to blend into society by mimicking good behavior. She's the life of the party, an excellent conversationalist, so fun to be around. She is popular in her sphere, so much so that you often feel crazy for even considering confronting her or warning others about her—because who would believe you? If you complain to someone else about her belittling behavior, the confidant is usually shocked, only knowing the predator when she is "on." This is why it's hard to report predators because they so easily have manipulated most people in their lives. Others cannot fathom (nor do they want to) that their kindhearted neighbor is actually a predator in disguise.

- She is the victim. Even though she spends her life victimizing others, it's always someone else's fault. I remember one victim sticking up for the man who choked her and exploited her by saying, "He only did that because his first girlfriend really hurt him." Here he was choking his girlfriend, all the while convincing her it was because of a former relationship. Similarly, Predator Paige will blame you for her awful behavior: "It's your fault I lash out like this. It's your fault I have to hit you. If you'd only just comply and be submissive."

- She flatters. Predatory people are master manipulators, and they know how to lure people who struggle on the fringes. They exploit your weaknesses by paying attention, building you up, pretending kindness.

- She gives lavish gifts.

- She goes out of her way to choose the unchosen. She knows vulnerable people are more susceptible to coercion and control.

- She tells intimate secrets that she says are *only* for you to know, which makes you feel special. She grants special access or privileges to you, fostering a feeling of exclusivity. She uses this form of manipulation for a period of time before she lets you know who she really is. But by that time, you're trapped. She lured you through kindness, but harmed you through abuse and control.

- She is never, ever wrong. Predatory people will go to any length to avoid personal responsibility. Besides blaming the victim (see above), she cannot exist in a world where she has flaws or perceived sins. So she deflects. She makes anyone who brings up her actions into a heinous, callous villain.

- She has elaborate conspiracy theories about people out to get her in order to deflect the true things those people or groups of people have against her. She always has a carefully prepared explanation and excuse for getting caught.[1]

- She hates your boundaries. She will violate them, but if you lash back, she will ridicule you until you agree that having boundaries is evil. Shahida Arabi advises (in terms of a dating relationship), "When your 'no' always seems like a negotiation to someone you're dating, beware. This means you're in the presence of someone who does not respect your right to make your own choices and maintain your boundaries or values."[2]

- She may become violent. When she doesn't get her way, she pushes, shoves, hits, or harms you. Then it becomes your fault for being so stubborn.

- She treats strangers who don't conform to her wishes with contempt.

- She re-creates history, recalling an event where she was clearly in the wrong, and instead painting herself in a martyr light.

- She needs constant contact with you. She will often isolate you from others in order to gain complete access to you. She will monitor your whereabouts, constantly checking in. When she cannot account for you, she will freak out and ask a million questions about where you were, who you were with, and why you felt it necessary to "cheat" on her.[3]

Predator Paige gets away with her predatory behavior precisely because she's an expert at it. When I met my friend Jimmy Hinton (mentioned in the Narcissist Nolan chapter), he let me know something both haunting and frightening: Sexually predatory behavior is not a crime of convenience (a victim was in the right place at the right time), but a continual, honed practice. In other words, predators spend nearly every ounce of energy perfecting their predatory technique, until they become so good at it that it's nearly impossible to stop them. That's why sexually deviant predators tend to get away with dozens or even hundreds of violations—it's their full-time, practiced job.

Getting hooked by a predator, then, is not something to heap blame on yourself about. It's common because predatory people live in all strata of society, and they often look like average folks in the neighborhood.

THREE ENCOUNTERS WITH PREDATORS

Jenna had a close friend in ministry—Alia. Jenna and her husband, John, spent a lot of time with Alia and her husband, Bruce, a rare ministry friendship. Jenna babysat Alia's children, and they often shared life together.

Jenna shares, "When my husband was going through a difficult time, I began sharing with my friend about how upset John was. I shared things he shared with me, thinking that she and her husband would pray for him."

Instead, Alia used that information to reach out to John personally. "She pretended that she was 'sensing things' about what he was feeling," Jenna said. "That resulted in an emotional connection that became an affair. A few months later, John realized what had happened, and he cut ties with her. Of course, I was deeply wounded. He became deeply depressed. We went through intensive counseling and, thankfully, were surrounded by people who walked with us through it. God pursued us, and, because of him and friends who supported us to continue walking in our calling, we came back around to a place of health. It was a hard journey. The thing I occasionally struggle with is that my friend has never said she was sorry. She never expressed remorse (her husband even said she didn't). We cut ties with them many years ago. It surprises me at times how that wound gets pricked from time to time…and how much I wish I could have relied on our friendship. It has taken me until this year to allow women to get close to me. I'm finally making female friends again, so I can tell that a lot of healing has taken place."

Alia, like Predator Paige, found a weakness in John and exploited her insider knowledge, making a difficult situation far more painful. It's amazing how a short period of time (a month or so with a predator) takes years to overcome. This is the hallmark of a predator's footprint on your life. He or she stomps on you and then moves on, but you're left with the sole impression deeply imprinted into your own broken soul.

Janice met a male predator, Barnaby, through a business association. They shared a commonality in their careers, and Janice felt she was safe because their business revolved around ministry. Barnaby began to ask her questions about her marriage, particularly the places where Janice felt unfulfilled. He also shared his own misgivings and difficult moments from his marriage. In the circle of this kind of confidentiality, a friendship emerged—nothing more. But soon Barnaby started sending mildly explicit messages to Janice, seemingly testing her response. When she didn't recoil but gave in to the flattery he sent her way, he continued, but each message grew more explicit—even in the midst of discussing theology. He eventually pressed her for pictures of herself, then continued to push her for more online interaction. Wisely, Janice told her husband about Barnaby's antics, and she severed contact.

In retrospect, Janice realized that Barnaby used his position and his Christianity to worm his way into her life—all because initially she let her guard down. In the aftermath of all this mess, she battles depression, blames herself mercilessly, and retraces why it all mushroomed so quickly. Of course, she lives with regret, but she is also realizing the predatory nature of Barnaby, who seemed to target her and pursue her.

Callie met a woman who she never thought of as predatory. After all, this new friend Sophia seemed to revere Callie, putting her on a pedestal. "I now understand that this was a red flag—that those who elevate us to 'amazing' status before they've gotten to know us very well are the first to shove us off when we prove ourselves to be human. Sophia had a way of making me feel safe to open up to her, and I was in a vulnerable place at the time, so I know I shared

too much too quickly," Callie wrote. "She was my biggest cheerleader for a while, eager to help, quick to encourage, the first to celebrate my accomplishments and tell everyone how wonderful I was.
I knew she'd been hurt by a lot of people, but so had I, so I made up
my mind to not be one of 'those' friends."

After that, Sophia did something that really bothered Callie. "I
trusted that we had the kind of relationship where she would want
me to speak up. She'd always encouraged my attempts to be braver,
so she would understand how difficult it was for me to do this,
right?" Except that Sophia did not take it well. "Not only did she
not take responsibility for her actions, but she twisted things around,
so it became a case of me hurting her, and I felt like a terrible friend."

Callie thought they'd worked everything out in that moment,
but a shift happened in their relationship. "After that, I couldn't
seem to get it right with her. Instead of being my cheerleader, she
bragged about other friends. She knew I was struggling and had
started going to counseling, and I think that just gave her more to
work with. Suddenly, I felt like the messed-up one who had issues.
Every once in a while we'd have a nice connection, but anytime I
questioned her, her response left me feeling crazy or like I was overreacting. I finally had to let go of her."

Interestingly, Callie realized her gut had been right in the beginning. "One scary thing I realized is that I vividly remember thinking (on more than one occasion), *I hope I never cross her, because if I
do, I can see her turning on me pretty quickly.* I knew my role was to
be the kind, encouraging friend. As long as I played that role, we
were fine, but the moment I stepped out of it, things changed. I've
also had moments when I wondered if she was using me. (We were
in the same profession, and I was further down the road.)"

Callie still sees Sophia from time to time, but their interaction
remains strained and awkward. "If she were telling the story, she

would probably say I dropped her and she doesn't understand why. Sometimes I wonder if her version of the story is correct—that I overreacted and couldn't let go of our first conflict. But I guess that reveals how unhealthy our relationship was. I learned one other lesson from this experience as well: It forced me to examine how easily special attention sucks me in. Throw a little public praise in there, even if 'public' is a small group of friends, and I'm hooked. This is something I'm asking God to work on in me." Callie adds, "I am now leery of anyone who comes on strong very quickly."

Predators are the deadliest of friends. They are typically deceptive, wolves in sheep's clothing, pretending to befriend, but preying upon instead. They're charming, popular, and often fun to be around. As mentioned above, they employ passive aggression, guilt, and gaslighting to keep you in the friendship, even after you've realized their deception. You constantly feel that something's very wrong with you, or that something is not quite right, but you can't put your finger on it.

You typically don't realize you've befriended a predator until you're out of the relationship. The retrospect, though, is very hard to deal with, as you face questions about why in the world you entrusted yourself to that person, who then dominated your heart and mind.

What Does the Bible Say?

First, we must remember where all this behavior derives its strength from—our adversary. Satan's primary aim is to steal, kill, and destroy us (see John 10:10). His goal is also the predator's ambition—to steal our innocence, kill our will, and destroy our souls. While predators are not Satan, and they are solely responsible for their actions (they can't merely say, "The devil made me do it"), they act in tandem with the evil forces in this world. And in this world, our Enemy prowls: "Stay alert! Watch out for your great enemy, the devil. He prowls around like a roaring lion, looking for someone to devour. Stand firm against him, and be strong in your faith. Remember that your family of believers all over the world is going through the same kind of suffering you are" (1 Peter 5:8-9).

Peter's words to us about Satan are instructive when we interact with or encounter a predator. We must stay alert to, watch out for, and stand firm against predatory people. Jesus warns us, "Look, I am sending you out as sheep among wolves. So be as shrewd as snakes and harmless as doves" (Matthew 10:16). We must become discerning people who are no longer deceived by predatory people.

How do we do that? We can read books.[4] We remember the doctrine of original sin and peruse the Bible when it warns about predators. Jeremiah 5:26-29 comes to mind:

> "Among my people are wicked men who lie in wait for victims like a hunter hiding in a blind. They continually set traps to catch people. Like a cage filled with birds, their homes are filled with evil plots. And now they are great and rich. They are fat and sleek, and there is no limit to their wicked deeds. They refuse to provide justice to orphans and deny the rights of the poor. Should I not punish them for this?" says the LORD. "Should I not avenge myself against such a nation?"

The Bible is full of warnings against people like this, which is wholly instructive. But the latter part of this verse is also encouraging. God sees what predators do. They may be able to get away with their behavior, seemingly forever, but they will not ultimately prevail. On the other side, God's perfect justice will be swift and just. Although that's not entirely helpful right now when you're suffering in the midst of a predatory relationship or its aftermath, it's a truth you can tuck away in your heart.

Job encountered predatory people, and his descriptions help us discern the predators in our lives. "People who are at ease mock those in trouble. They give a push to people who are stumbling" (Job 12:5). Predators are comfortable mocking their prey, and they are skilled at knowing when someone is at their breaking point, pushing just a bit to send them careening off a precipice.

Predators also keep good records. "You write bitter accusations against me and bring up all the sins of my youth" (Job 13:26). Not only do they write accusatory words, but the intent is always destruction: "How long will you torture me? How long will you try to crush me with your words?" (Job 19:2).

Often these predators masquerade as men and women of God, stealing the innocence of others. Consider The Message's rendition of Jeremiah 29:23:

> "Those two men, sex predators and prophet-impostors, got what they deserved. They pulled every woman they got their hands on into bed—their neighbors' wives, no less—and preached lies claiming it was my Message. I never sent those men. I've never had anything to do with them." God's Decree. "They won't get away with a thing. I've witnessed it all."

God's beautiful sovereignty gives us solace. He sees. He knows. He will make things right. In writing that, I know I run the risk of backlash—because where was God when someone perpetrated against us? As a victim of childhood sexual abuse at the hands of two predators much stronger than me, I have asked this question, but haven't yet found a satisfying answer. Of course, I can say I learned a lot, and that my healing of this travesty has made for amazing ministry opportunities. But I would be lying if I said I'm happy it happened. And I'm sure you're not happy you've encountered and experienced a predatory relationship. Yet the truth remains, despite the questions, that God will eventually make things right. It's a tenuous hope, but it is assured.

How did predators come into being? Why do they seem to move from bad to worse? For that, we have to look at Paul's discourse in Romans 1:24-32, a well-known passage about people, sin, and the impact it has on their lives. Paul writes,

> So God abandoned them to do whatever shameful things their hearts desired. As a result, they did vile and degrading things with each other's bodies. They traded the truth about God for a lie. So they worshiped and served the things God created instead of the Creator himself, who is worthy of eternal praise! Amen. That is why God abandoned them to their shameful desires. Even the women turned against the natural way to have sex and instead indulged in sex with each other. And the men, instead of having normal sexual relations with women, burned with lust for each other. Men did shameful things with other men, and as a result of this sin, they suffered within themselves the penalty they deserved. Since they thought it foolish to acknowledge God, he abandoned them to their foolish thinking and let them do things that should never be done. Their lives became full of every kind of wickedness, sin, greed, hate, envy, murder, quarreling, deception, malicious behavior, and gossip. They are backstabbers, haters of God, insolent, proud, and boastful. They invent new ways of sinning, and they disobey their parents. They refuse to understand, break their promises, are heartless, and have no mercy. They know God's justice requires that those who do these things deserve to die, yet they do them anyway. Worse yet, they encourage others to do them, too.

We see here that God allows for people to dive headlong into themselves, influencing the way they act and think. If someone wants to indulge in egregious sinful behavior, God permits it. But there is always a consequence. When we worship only ourselves and live solely for our agendas and "happiness," God gives us over to a depraved mind. His hand of protection is removed, and he allows us to wallow in our sinful behavior. Notice some of the "fruit" of this kind of continual sin: deception, malicious behavior, boasting, promise breaking, heartlessness, and mercilessness—all traits of a predator.

You may argue, "But my predator is a Christian!" Really? To this I refer back to Jesus's admonition about fruit in Matthew 7:15-20:

> Beware of false prophets who come disguised as harmless sheep but are really vicious wolves. You can identify them by their fruit, that is, by the way they act. Can you pick grapes from thornbushes, or figs from thistles? A good tree produces good fruit, and a bad tree produces bad fruit. A good tree can't produce bad fruit, and a bad tree can't produce good fruit. So every tree that does not produce good fruit is chopped down and thrown into the fire. Yes, just as you can identify a tree by its fruit, so you can identify people by their actions.

Someone who joyfully pursues Christ has good, discernible fruit. Someone who consistently harms people, although they use all the correct Christian language and attend church like the rest of us, does not produce good fruit. Maybe it's time we stop giving people who say all the right words a hall pass for predatory behavior. Instead, let's be cautious when we meet someone with big words accompanied by bad actions.

We see the remorse of God and his grief as he looks at mankind's propensity to prey on each other. How he responds is instructive: "The Lord observed the extent of human wickedness on the earth, and he saw that everything they thought or imagined was consistently and totally evil. So the LORD was sorry he had ever made them and put them on the earth. It broke his heart" (Genesis 6:5-6). Did you see that? Wickedness on this grand scale breaks the heart of God. Because not only does it harm his children, but it also represents a myriad of sins against him. So God is broken twice by a predator's sin. In light of that, we have the empathy of God as we try to navigate the aftereffects of a predator.

What can we do when we encounter a predator?

Separate. As I shared in the narcissist chapter, Paul's encouragement remains the same. Have nothing to do with them. Cut ties. Let go of correspondence. Unfollow them from social media. Block them on your phone. You may think it's mean to do this, but it's actually kind—to yourself. You are also (possibly) preventing others from being abused by creating a firm boundary of no contact. So often predators receive no consequences for their actions, but you separating is one way they can feel the weight of their behavior.

Report. Ephesians 5:11 instructs, "Take no part in the worthless deeds of evil and darkness; instead, expose them." If you see others being reeled into a predator's trap, warn them. If the predator has committed a crime, report it to the proper authorities (the police, not your local church). Churches are great at providing spiritual counseling, but they are not equipped to handle civil or criminal cases. If the predator has not necessarily broken laws but has acted unethically, you may have recourse in reporting them to their association or place of employment. Tread lightly before you do this, and please consult a lawyer.

Don't be a savior. If you do, you'll have to continue to "save" a predator. Proverbs 19:19 warns us that "hot-tempered people must pay the penalty. If you rescue them once, you will have to do it again." Similarly, don't ever help a predator conceal his or her true self. They're masters at reputation management and often appeal to people in their inner circle to do their damage control. Rescuing a predator only empowers them to prey on more victims.

Reevaluate pity. Predators are skilled at enticing others to pity them. According to an article about sociopathic people in the church, "Pity is another socially valuable response, and it should be reserved for innocent people who are in genuine pain or who have fallen on misfortune. If, instead, you find yourself often pitying someone who consistently hurts you or other people, and who actively campaigns for your sympathy, the chances are close to 100 percent that you are dealing with a sociopath."[5]

Reform how you think about respect. In the same article, the author encourages,

> If necessary, redefine your concept of respect. Too often, we mistake fear for respect, and the more fearful we are of someone, the more we view him or her as deserving of our respect. To mistake fear for respect is to ensure your own victimization. Let us use our big human brains to overpower our animal tendency to bow to predators, so we can disentangle the reflexive confusion of anxiety and awe. In a perfect world, human respect would be an automatic reaction only to those who are strong, kind, and morally courageous. The person who profits from frightening you is not likely to be any of these.[6]

Pray. The Psalms are full of examples of people praying for release from predators. Consider this: "See how many enemies I have and how viciously they hate me! Protect me! Rescue my life from them! Do not let me be disgraced, for in you I take refuge. May integrity and honesty protect me, for I put my hope in you" (Psalm 25:19-21). Be blatantly honest with the Almighty about the people who are harming you. Ask for help. Lament your lot. God is near to those who call on him with the truth of their painful situation. He hears our cries. Perhaps you've prayed but you can't seem to find breakthrough. You may need to ask a friend or two to pray alongside you. In the circle of positive community, you can begin the process of healing.

Get counsel and counseling. Proverbs 15:22 encourages, "Plans go wrong for lack of advice; many advisers bring success." As in asking for corporate prayer, seeking the advice of wiser, older friends will give you the perspective you need to separate from a predator. But beyond that, it's important to realize that predators leave prey in their swath of destruction, and often those prey (you!) have been traumatized by past interactions. In this case, it's wise to seek professional counseling, particularly with someone specializing in PTSD and/or trauma therapy.

AM I PREDATOR PAIGE?

As I mentioned in the narcissist chapter, if you're worried about being predatory, you're most likely not. Predators are seldom self-aware. They don't introspect, wondering if they're hurting others. They're consumed with how they can harm others, and their consciences are seared. If you've apologized for your actions when you hurt someone, or you've asked God to please help you be more patient with people, chances are you're not Predator Paige. If you're worried, ask your community because your closest relationships will be able to tell you. If your close friend seems afraid to speak about your actions, if he or she is reticent to bring up a negative trait of yours, pay attention. Assure your friend that you absolutely want to know. And if their words ring stingingly true, take a step back, breathe deeply, and apologize sincerely.

Predator Paige represents the deadliest of friendships. She slays with her tongue and her actions, and, in some cases, murders those she loves. It is not your job to reform her. It is hers. Your recourse is to separate and heal, entrusting your heart to the One who sees it all.

4

CONMAN CONNOR

"A Heart That Plots Evil"

When Grayson shared the need, I listened. I admired his heart for people who were broken, praised him for his guts to inconvenience himself for their sakes. He corralled several mutual friends into his ministry, asked for advice. He was a long-standing friend, so there were no red flags. We'd known him as someone who helped people, and we'd shared life together on numerous occasions, deeply connected. We broke bread together and dreamed.

Eventually, his ministry endeavor started showing cracks. I'd heard a few harrowing stories of abuse, exploitation, and under-handed business practices. Initially, I dismissed them, assuming positive intent of my friend. I had never known him to be exploitive. Surely, none of these rumors were true.

Except that they were. And as my husband and I began to address the issues, we learned the truth. Grayson was running an elaborate scam—all to his benefit—on the backs of the poorest of the poor. All that history in our friendship rushed back to me. With new eyes, I was able to see the fissures of his personality, the other indications of his heart over the years. He moved swiftly from job to job. He always seemed to pursue new business ventures that panned out for a while and then spectacularly failed. He cut corners in his personal finances and didn't seem bothered that he did so. He did little cheats that ended up snowballing into this recent endeavor.

The Scripture is true: "If you are faithful in little things, you will be faithful in large ones. But if you are dishonest in little things, you won't be honest with greater responsibilities" (Luke 16:10). And if those decisions involve money, you'll end up hurting not only yourself, but also those around you. Jesus reminded us of this important truth: "No one can serve two masters. For you will hate one and love the other; you will be devoted to one and despise the other. You cannot serve both God and be enslaved to money" (Matthew 6:24).

The entire Bible is replete with wisdom about money, how we handle it, and how it affects our hearts, but it also cautions us to never exploit others in our management of it. Unfortunately, this kind of sin touches many of us. It certainly affected our livelihood.

When I met Elizabeth, I immediately liked her. She presented herself as a victim of several dishonorable (in her words) people in her life. Being attracted to victims and longing to make things right, I immediately (unwisely!) jumped into a relationship with her. She corralled several others like me and began telling stories that became wilder and more outlandish. And oh, the people who hurt her! They were the devil incarnate. Conspiracy theories abounded. She moved several times, each time being taken advantage of by companies and people. She suffered from an incurable injury, only to find out it was curable by surgery. Friends rallied to her and raised money for her surgery, but we were never quite sure if she had it. Come to find out, most of her life had been elaborately fabricated—all while money flowed her way.

When we met Jacob, he became the answer to our money prayers. In retrospect, we were ripe to be preyed upon. Ready to leave for France as missionaries, our unsold house felt like an albatross around our necks. Our fear made us overlook red flags. He'd been referred to us from someone in our global prayer gathering at church, and he was a church member, so we didn't think twice about setting up a meeting with him. Friendly, charming, disarming—all those words described him as my husband and I forged a relationship with him.

He didn't ask right away, but eventually he shared how he could help us with our yet-to-be-sold house. He would buy it from us! He brought us dinner from a local Italian restaurant and explained everything. Around our table, he reminded us that he worked for a local mortgage company and that he would take care of everything. When we signed the papers, everything was notarized and "legal."

We continued our friendship as we left for France. He would check in on us occasionally, and we would share what new things were happening as we planted a church. After a while, though, he stopped contacting us. His ex-wife e-mailed me, warning us about him—that he wasn't a trustworthy person, and he had defrauded others. So swayed by the earnest charisma of Jacob, I naively dismissed her e-mail.

Around Christmas, we received a call from our bank that held our old mortgage. They demanded to know why we weren't making our mortgage payment. "We sold our home months ago," my husband said. That one line inaugurated an extensive investigation into the life of Jacob. As it turned out, he created paperwork that said we owned the mortgage, but he owned the title of our home. The legitimate papers we did sign and got notarized were never sent. Our only recourse was to evict him from our house, that he had now destroyed, and let the house go into foreclosure. It's a long, boring, and complicated story, and I've shared it in other places, but I wanted to share it here so you understand that we are all susceptible to Conman Connor.

In the church, we are prone to grant trust without first seeing trustworthiness in action. We had never met Jacob prior to our prayer team friend's introduction. We had the deadly combination of fear (our house won't sell) and blind trust (he goes to our church). We learned the hard way that people who say they are Christ followers might just be scoundrels.

David Modic emphasizes that everyone has the potential to be scammed. The false belief that it's only the older generation that falls for conmen numbs people into thinking their intelligence will prevent it. "If it did," he wrote, "then better educated people and older people would be less likely to fall for scams. And that is not supported by my research."[1]

His research highlights the kind of traits scam victims share. "Some of these traits—like a lack of self-control—we would probably recognise [sic] as dangerous. But others—a trust in authority, a desire to act in the same way as our friends, or a tendency to act in a consistent way—we might think of as good characteristics."[2]

All these traits mimic how we tend to act in the church. We trust authority. We love to fit in with our Christian friends. We are consistent in our choices. All these positive traits make it easy for a conman like Jacob to swoop in and take advantage.

Maria Konnikova, who wrote *The Confidence Game: Why We Fall for It…Every Time,* agrees: "One study of con victims found that two factors seemed to play a major role in which emotionally susceptible people, in particular, fell prey to an unscrupulous actor: they were more optimistic and more religious. In other words, they believed things could get better, and they believed that greater forces could play a role in that improvement."[3] Which is why Conman Connor seems to flourish in our Christian environments.

TRAITS

Conman Connor behaves this way:

- Conman Connor shares a marriage of traits with Narcissist Nolan and Predator Paige, though his intent isn't to steal your soul; it's to take your money.
- He is charming, irresistibly so.
- The two of you share a mutual friend, and that friend thinks the world of him.
- He may say he has an important job—doctor, lawyer, researcher.
- He first invites you into a business endeavor that has zero risk.
- He loves and displays nice things—an expensive watch, a nice car, a well-decorated home—though a conman can also exist in every level of society.
- He comes across as having hidden, exclusive knowledge.
- His pleas for your monetary involvement are always time sensitive. It must be invested now before the opportunity passes.
- Later you find out he has many victims and many scams running simultaneously.
- He cries easily.
- He distorts his image, sometimes even doctoring photos to make himself appear more attractive.
- He name-drops.
- He makes up degrees and awards, sometimes to the extent that they're printed off and placed in frames in his office.
- He has pictures of himself next to prominent people displayed in his home or office.

- He has long tales about being wronged by someone else; his story is so persuasive you feel indignant and want to help him.

- For a period of time, he would do anything for you. He will exhaust himself for you, bend over backward helping you.

- He believes you should be grateful for this amazing opportunity he is sacrificing to send your way.

- Initially, he comes across as unassuming and humble— someone you would want to help.

- He likes to be perceived as an expert, and he hangs around other experts to bolster this perception.

- He is excessively skilled at gaining your confidence, hence the term "confidence man." He does this so well, you're willing to defend him when he's caught for another scam.

- He's skilled at mimicry. He reads any and every situation, then fits right in, mimicking the language and behavior of those around him. In short, he's a chameleon.

- He appeals to your deepest desires, something that blinds you to rational thinking. In our case it was "sell our house before we leave the country."

- He flat out asks for money.

- He sometimes disappears for long periods of time with no explanation as to why.

- He's Teflon. Nothing seems to stick to him.

- He moves fast when it comes to intimacy. One day you didn't know him, the next he is inviting you into his inner circle, sharing extremely personal stories, and eliciting equally personal stories from you.

- He is relentless in asking you to participate in his venture. He pesters.
- You get the feeling you'll lose the relationship unless you do what he says (give your money to him).
- He treats you like a friend, but deep down you know you're a prospect.
- He pretends you are closer, more intimate, even though the relationship is shallow.
- He contacts you out of the blue when you've had little or no contact for several years. Early into the conversation, he tells you about this exciting opportunity.
- He is a smooth talker and can alleviate any objection or fear you may articulate.
- He is usually overly polite.
- He possesses an uncanny ability to understand you, discern your thoughts—almost like he's reading your mind.
- He offends easily, and when he is, he reacts aggressively. (How dare you question my motives and integrity!)
- He is manipulative and always has a comeback to your objections.
- He does not love your *no,* but he adores your *yes.*
- If you reject his business venture, you are rejecting him, and he will swiftly move on to his next relationship.
- He appeals to your greed.
- He can't really explain what he does, but his lifestyle

reflects wealth, and you can't figure out how this person with so much free time gets his money.

- He lies often and easily. Nothing he says is true, and often the lies are stupid lies that don't matter, like what he bought at the store yesterday. Lying has become his native language so much so that he cannot even discern when he lies or doesn't lie. In other words, everything coming out of his mouth is a lie.

- He lives for his reputation. He impugns anyone who threatens it with incredulity.

- He can overreact and threaten suicide if things don't go his way.

- You get the feeling he believes he's better and smarter than everyone else.

- He intimidates people, but with deference.

- He leverages your relationship as a means to pressure you to part from your money.

- He appeals to people's need for financial gain by assuring them that they are good people who deserve the nicer things in life.

One of the most insidious abilities of Conman Connor is his keen awareness of people when they're feeling low. It's like he has a built in fear-o-meter, and when someone tips it, he swoops in. We certainly gave in to fear when our house hadn't sold, making us a perfect mark. Konnikova continues, "A victim isn't necessarily foolish or greedy. A victim is simply more emotionally vulnerable at the exact moment the confidence artist approaches. Risk taking and impulsivity need not be stable aspects of our personalities; they are intimately tied to where we find ourselves emotionally at any given point."[4] That's why Conman Connor is exploitive, and it's also why we must be cautious when we're emotionally fearful or drained. In those states, we are more apt to be taken advantage of.

My three examples above may not be relatable to you. Or perhaps you don't know someone who checks everything off the list above. We often think of conmen and conwomen as folks who are featured on the CNBC show *American Greed*—white-collar criminals bilking retirees of millions. We think of Bernie Madoff and the swath of destruction he created. But I'd like to offer a slightly different variation of Conman Connor, one that is less criminal. What if he is simply someone who is interested in having a relationship with you because you can give him money? And what if he's not conning you out of it, but offering you a business opportunity? Certainly, not all multilevel marketing platforms exploit relationships (I certainly have friends who navigate their online businesses with integrity), but perhaps you've encountered a friend who comes out of the woodwork of your past, wanting to share an exciting opportunity with you. Anytime money moves in and through a relationship, you have a situation ripe for possible exploitation.

FRIENDS AND MONEY

Lyria had a very close friend, Marta, whom she met at church. Lyria and her husband joined the same small group as Marta and her husband. Over several years, they become very close—the kind of friendship that holds each other accountable and encourages each to grow in their faith. They loved spending time together—Marta was one of Lyria's favorite people. Lyria moved, but still she kept in contact with Marta via e-mail. "When we came back," Lyria writes, "we heard from them that there had been a dispute between the leadership and her extended family. She sided with her family and left the church, but not without great sorrow given the ways they loved and were loved in our church family." Because of the split, they weren't in close fellowship anymore, but they still maintained their friendship.

"I loved and appreciated Marta and missed her companionship," Lyria writes. "I hadn't heard from her in a long time, maybe a year, when she called me out of the blue. I was thrilled to hear from her, and our conversation was very joyous at first—like a reunion, getting caught up on news, and I felt very hopeful. And then she told me the reason for her call. She was selling a health product and was wondering if I would be interested in purchasing from her. My heart dropped. I was so very sad—and this was also after several friends had joined the same company! I was already annoyed with this company that was turning my friendships into business opportunities, but this was the clincher for me. It was pretty devastating considering all we'd shared and the depth of our friendship. I said no, and our phone call ended shortly. I actually had to work on forgiving her over time, because we would run into each other afterward, and I kept feeling let down by her."

Candace had a longtime friend from elementary through high school that started selling a product after college. Candace writes, "I went to a couple events with her and ended up buying $200 worth of merchandise on a payment plan. From that day on, the only time she reached out to me was to discuss payments. When I would try to connect with her outside of business, she was always busy or didn't return my calls or texts. I felt very used and taken advantage of."

It's important to note that not all friends use their friends to sell things. Candace continues, "On the other hand, I have another friend I've known just as long who started selling with one of those companies, and I was a little nervous to mix business with friendship again. But not only has her product worked great for me, it has not interfered with our friendship at all…to the contrary, it's even strengthened it. I think the difference is that the second friend has a clear mission and purpose for why she is doing it, and it's something I greatly respect! The second friend also made a point to contact and connect with me with no mention of her business unless I brought it up, which gives me comfort and confidence in continuing business with her!"

Emily encountered a friend who constantly pitched her product. "It hurts my heart deeply as I know with each pitch, I'm a means to an end. I've had to weigh my role with her: Am I here to support her need for financial support, or do I refuse and deal with that result—whatever it may be? It's tough to know when you're serving another in obedience to God and when you're just a paycheck."

One viral blog post summed up a blogger's frustration with the constant asking for money, particularly over social media. She laments, "I'm not going to try the skincare. I'm not giving it thirty days. I could put Elmer's glue on my face for thirty days, then take a picture and see a major difference. I have Photoshop, too."[5]

Christianity Today editor Kate Shelnutt wrote an essay about this dilemma. She writes,

> When I began asking my friends directly about MLM [multilevel marketing], they were relieved to finally open up about something so pervasive yet rarely discussed. I heard stories from people who cut off relationships due to the sales pressure. Many admitted to blocking Facebook friends whose updates constantly centered on their company and the new sales levels they reached. Several stopped speaking to friends—even siblings—who continued to ask them to buy, or to get in on the 'opportunity' to sell, even after they had declined.[6]

Crown Ministries addresses this tendency for people, particularly in multilevel companies, to take advantage of their friends. "The concept of multilevel direct sales is not wrong, but quite often its practices are. Anytime a Christian must trick another person into listening to a sales pitch while promising fellowship, it is wrong! Anytime a Christian is more interested in selling a product than in ministering to someone else's needs, that person is in service to money and not to God! Each believer must test his or her own attitudes before the Lord."[7]

And that's what we'll do as we explore what the Bible says about this kind of money-centric friendship.

WHAT THE BIBLE SAYS

The Old Testament prophet Jeremiah speaks often to the excesses of Israel. Yes, they worshipped idols. Yes, they strayed from God's covenant. Yes, they forgot the faithfulness of God. But one of the most telling things their apostasy manifested itself as was plain old greed. Jeremiah writes, "From the least to the greatest, their lives are ruled by greed. From prophets to priests, they are all frauds" (Jeremiah 6:13). Note how Jeremiah mentions greed and fraud in the same breath. A conman is ruled by greed. Jeremiah further warns, "Like a partridge that hatches eggs she has not laid, so are those who get their wealth by unjust means. At midlife they will lose their riches; in the end, they will become poor old fools" (17:11). Interestingly, studies show that people who harm others tend to get found out as they age. In other words, their ability to con and cajole gets found out, and less and less people tolerate their antics, which confirms the scripture about losing their riches.

According to a recent article about aging narcissists (and remember, conmen tend toward narcissism or sociopathic tendencies), "they tend to dominate their social environment using brutal, covert situational abuse tactics, but as their social circle starts to narrow inevitably during old age, they are able to find fewer and fewer people emotionally and psychologically capable of providing care due to the narcissistic predator's unquenchable thirst to abuse."[8]

The book of Proverbs has much to say about folks who take money from others in unscrupulous ways. "Wealth from get-rich-quick schemes quickly disappears; wealth from hard work grows over time" (13:11). I find it fascinating that get-rich-quick schemes are as old as history; people have been pursuing and promising them for millennia, and yet we still see the same patterns today. Part of that is our own sinful nature, longing to have our financial problems solved in a simple, easy way. Our laziness fuels our greed. It would be much nicer to win a lottery than spend a lifetime working, so we bite when a friend tells us of a surefire opportunity. The problem is twofold: We get taken, but the person "taking" us is also harmed in that he or she gets away with sin, and that continued foray into sinful behavior eventually shipwrecks them.

This kind of debased behavior degenerates into taking advantage of the poor or flattering those in power with that ill-gotten gain. "A person who gets ahead by oppressing the poor or by showering gifts on the rich will end in poverty" (22:16). Proverbs sums up how we should live in the shadow of a world caught by greed: "The trustworthy person will get a rich reward, but a person who wants quick riches will get into trouble. Showing partiality is never good, yet some will do wrong for a mere piece of bread. Greedy people try to get rich quick but don't realize they're headed for poverty" (28:20-22).

In light of this, it's imperative to separate from your friend ensnared in this kind of friend funding, but perhaps not permanently. It's worth a long talk, appealing to your friend's sense of fairness and decency (in the case of someone wanting you to constantly buy things or join their downline). But if your friend resembles more the people I first mentioned in this chapter, folks who are outright defrauding others, your recourse will be more severe.

In our situation, we talked to the first man and then warned others who wanted to donate to his "ministry." We prosecuted the man who stole our house. (He conveniently declared bankruptcy before we won our settlement, then moved away to defraud retirees of their pensions.) I uncovered the deception of my third friend and cautiously warned others not to trust her. Sometimes with Conman Connor, we have to alert and report so that they will be caught and other innocent victims can be saved.

Lest you think that folks who intermarry friendship with financial greed is a minor problem, note this list Paul creates about folks who are far from the kingdom of God.

> Don't you realize that those who do wrong will not inherit the Kingdom of God? Don't fool yourselves. Those who indulge in sexual sin, or who worship idols, or commit adultery, or are male prostitutes, or practice homosexuality, or are thieves, or greedy people, or drunkards, or are abusive, or cheat people—none of these will inherit the Kingdom of God. Some of you were once like that. But you were cleansed; you were made holy; you were made right with God by calling on the name of the Lord Jesus Christ and by the Spirit of our God (1 Corinthians 6:9-11).

Did you catch that? Idol worshippers and prostitutes are equated with thieves and those who cheat others.

The frustrating part of all this is that many of these conmen find homes in the church. Why? Because Christians tend to give the benefit of the doubt. We trust easily. Even if a person has a background of taking advantage of others, if she has said, "That was my old life; I've repented. I have a new story—a story of redemption," we have a hard time saying her words aren't true. We love redemptive stories! But this passage serves as a warning that there are conmen in

Christian clothing, sometimes even clergy clothing. We must be alert. And we must realize that letting them continue to sin in this way does not hurt only them as they're handed over to their own devices, but it also harms the community, particularly the vulnerable ones living within it. We must speak out for their sake.

An abusive friendship based on financial exchange is not really a friendship in the first place. And if that friend continues to take advantage of other believers, she is guilty of the same sin of the money changers in the temple, the scene where we see Jesus at his angriest. "Then, going over to the people who sold doves, he told them, 'Get these things out of here. Stop turning my Father's house into a marketplace!'" (John 2:16). Marketing and ministry, in this case, do not mix.

What happens, though, if Conman Connor skips town? (This was the case with the man who stole our house. We learned about his movements only in retrospect.) We have to trust that God knows and sees it all. He loves the poor and the oppressed, and he will take up their cause.

Micah 2:1-3 has some sober warnings for Conman Connor:

> What sorrow awaits you who lie awake at night, thinking up evil plans. You rise at dawn and hurry to carry them out, simply because you have the power to do so. When you want a piece of land, you find a way to seize it. When you want someone's house, you take it by fraud and violence. You cheat a man of his property, stealing his family's inheritance. But this is what the LORD says: "I will reward your evil with evil; you won't be able to pull your neck out of the noose. You will no longer walk around proudly, for it will be a terrible time."

In the case of our conman, he dropped dead of a heart attack at a very young age. And even if he hadn't, the Lord would eventually lay bare all of his sins, whether in this life or the next. Jesus reminds us that secrets are never really secrets: "For all that is secret will eventually be brought into the open, and everything that is concealed will be brought to light and made known to all" (Luke 8:17). Even so, we must always bend toward what my husband, Patrick, calls eschatological living—living in light of the new heavens and the new earth. Some of our predatory friendships have the possibility of reconciliation on the other side—and that brings hope.

AM I CONMAN CONNOR?

If you're a swindler and conman, you're most likely not going to pick up a book about deadly friendships. But in the softer side of this, friend, do evaluate whether you use your friends for financial gain, particularly in your business. I've seen this with authors (usually ones with only one book). They tell everyone about their book, introduce it into every single conversation. Their social media is constantly permeated with it, and they ask their friends often to buy it or promote it. While it's normal to hawk your wares, and it's commendable that you're working to make a living, it's never okay to take advantage of your friendships, leveraging them to increase your bottom line. A simple question of a good friend can confirm or deny that you're acting this way. Be brave enough to ask.

If you've encountered a Conman Connor in the extreme sense (in that he bilked you out of lots of money) or the milder sense (your friend only pursues you if you buy her exciting product), chances are you've experienced some form of predation. Whether you separate permanently or in the short term, remember to take the necessary time to heal, and be cautious whenever you find yourself in a vulnerable spot. Conman Connor thrives best in vulnerable places.

5

Tempter Trevor

"Feet That Race to Do Wrong"

Daniella's sheer personality wooed me toward her. She was popular, talkative, and moved comfortably in circles where I never could. I wanted to be "guilty by association" because she put forth a life I had longed for. My own insecurities made me her easy target, and she swooped in and brought me into her inner circle. It was heady at first, intoxicating.

But eventually I started noticing things about Daniella's life that didn't add up. The circles under her eyes after an evening of drinking a lot. Coarse talk that occasionally spilled out. Lies—seemingly little white lies at first—grew. She gossiped like crazy, so much so that I worried she'd also share my disclosures with others.

For a year or so I contemplated whether I should stay in the relationship. Never one to drink much, her bent toward overimbibing didn't tempt me, but her dogged pursuit up the ladder of success did. I'm an achiever at heart, and while there's a lot of good in being an achiever (I get a lot done), there's something insidious about that trait as well. I like to succeed. So when she asked me to cut corners, bend the truth, and cover for her—all under the guise of success—I faced a painful dilemma.

I loved her. We were years-long friends. But when she asked me to violate my conscience, I knew I needed to part ways. In the aftermath of it all, I realized that true, good friends don't ask you to violate your conscience. They do not pull you away from your ideals or your desire to follow Christ. They don't undermine your pursuit of holiness or actively woo you away from the kinds of choices you'll be proud of.

Peer pressure also plays into Tempter Trevor's ways. And Tempter Trevor actually may be *Tempter Trevors* because he gathers other friends, showing you that everything is cool, and how you don't need to be so legalistic about everything.

I encountered this in high school soon after I became a Christian. I started noticing that a lot of my Christian friends were going to parties (nothing wrong with that per se), getting drunk, and then doing things they would later regret. A few in the circle actively made fun of me, calling me a Pharisee, and actively undermining my choice to stay away. Having several Tempter Trevors in my life at that time, I did have this insatiable desire to be accepted by them all, to just quit being so tightly wound and have some fun. What they did appeared to be outlandishly enjoyable, and I struggled with my decisions.

I faltered several times. I joined in (I was terrified of alcohol then, having grown up around alcoholics) by attending parties, but I seldom drank. My friends seemed to be saying, *This is what people do to have fun, and you are not fun if you don't participate.* Eventually, I found a new group of friends who sought ways to have fun that didn't involve premarital sex and drinking.

Tempter Trevor subtly or not so subtly undermines wise choices, good habits, and Jesus-like attitudes. He fuels your arguments with your spouse, tempts you to betray your ethics, sucks you into gossip vortexes, and cherishes his ability to coerce you toward regrettable words or actions. When you push against this friend (in an attempt to better yourself), he often responds with anger and belittling.

TRAITS

Tempter Trevor behaves this way:

- He undermines you, particularly when you're gaining victory in a certain area of life.

- He tends to pursue friends who have different morals than you do. His circle is full of people you wouldn't normally associate with.

- He insults your choices, calling them quaint or antiquated.

- He actively pulls you away from resolutions you've made. If you're trying to lose weight, he offers molten chocolate cake. If you're reducing your alcohol intake, he tempts you with a mojito—or three.

- He asks you to do things that directly violate your conscience, and he seems to think nothing of it.

- He constantly questions your beliefs, not in an I-want-to-understand-your-faith way, but in an interrogative, undermining way.

- He coerces you to participate in his excessive lifestyle.

- He praises the benefits of his lifestyle, exaggerating his joy and underemphasizing the pitfalls.

- When you're around him, you're transported back to high school and those times you felt peer pressure.

- When you're with him, you often find yourself in compromising positions.

- Instead of respecting your faith and choices, he seeks to undermine them.

- You find yourself morphing into him and his choices, rather than you influencing him toward better decisions. (The youth group illustration of the chair is illustrative. When someone stands on a chair and another is on the ground, it is nearly impossible to pull the grounded person up to the chair, but it's easy for the grounded person to pull the chair-standing person to their level on the ground.)

- On one hand, you don't like yourself when you're around him, but you also kind of actually do like the crazy adventure and adrenaline you feel when you're around him.

- He talks negatively about anyone that doesn't go along with him, and you worry that he'll do the same with you if you don't join in.

- His friendship is a gateway to a more exciting circle of friends, so you feel pressure from him to be accepted in order to be welcomed by all.

- His opinion is the only correct one. He will spend a lot of time sharing his views, but when you assert yours, he shuts you down.

- He is passive aggressive when you don't participate in all the "fun."

- You get the feeling he's mining you for secrets, not to know you, but to use those against you later.

- He lies to others in front of you.

- He doesn't seem to feel bad for asking/forcing you to overextend yourself.

- He instills panic in you; when you're around him, you worry you'll lose him if you don't do everything he wants/demands.

- He dominates every conversation with you, and he constantly interrupts.

- He brings out the worst part of yourself, the part of you you've been working on with Jesus to reform.

- His goals in life and yours are often at odds.

- If you were choosing the best possible friend you needed to grow in your relationship with God, you would not choose him; instead, you would avoid him. (And if you had a child in high school that had this friend, you would advise your child to stay away.)

- He creates an atmosphere of friendship where you feel like you have to compete for his attention.

- He doesn't seem to see your internal wrestling about making bad choices. Instead, he salves your fears by saying it's no big deal.

- He craves excitement.

ENCOUNTERS WITH TEMPTER TREVORS

One woman, "Feeling Stuck," wrote this to Carolyn Hax, an advice columnist for *The Washington Post*:

There is a group of women with whom I've taken weekend trips once or twice a year. Back in May, we tossed around possible trip ideas for the summer. Nothing was decided. I saw two of these friends (the third lives in another state) a couple times in June and July, and none of us brought up a discussion of a trip. Fast-forward to when I opened my Instagram feed to see the three of them on vacation together. I was floored and devastated. None had invited me or told me about it.

She wrote that she worked through her pain and the feelings of abandonment, then commented, "I came to realize these friendships were based in superficiality and heavy drinking, and weren't healthy for me."[1]

Faith shares a story about being a new Christian, alone and living in a new city and state. She writes,

I was wrestling with my faith and sexuality. Hesitant at best to go to church, I opted to attend a faith-based recovery program. I soon connected with a woman named Wendy. She privately disclosed that she was a lesbian after I had shared in our closed group that I was trying to come to terms with my sexual identity and faith. Her disclosure sealed our friendship in quick-setting cement. We became inseparable. Texting frequently throughout the day and spending all our free time watching movies, going out and getting drunk and "innocently snuggling." Wendy kept pushing the boundaries and toying with my emotions, especially concerning since I was alone and fresh out of a long-term relationship. Her gestures seemed normal to me at the time. Eventually, we had sex and started viewing porn together. When I got to Step three of the twelve steps (we made a decision to turn our wills over to the care of God), I read Romans 12:1: "Therefore, I urge you brothers, in view of God's mercy, to offer your bodies as living sacrifices, holy and pleasing to God—this is your spiritual act of worship." I recognized I had a problem. Hooking up with Wendy, viewing porn, and getting drunk were keeping me from knowing God. This was my first act of surrender to break off the relationship with her and commit to one year of sexual purity as I wrestled with my faith and sexuality.

Hannah's encounter with Tempter Trevor started with one word:

Happy. I never thought this word would help guide me down a long and painful road. From the first time I met Maria, there was something dangerously attractive about her. She was fun, colorful, edgy. My definition of a cool mom. Amidst the sea of minivans and sippy cups, she was different. She had beautiful children and would regularly gush about how much she adored her husband.

During that time, Hannah's marriage felt bland, but the love Maria had for her husband seemed irresistible. Hannah continues, "As we grew closer, I opened up about the struggles in my marriage."

"I just want you to be happy, whatever that means for you," Maria repeated frequently during their conversations.

"She would share things her husband would do for her while criticizing mine for not doing the same. And I began to agree. I wasn't happy. I deserved more. My complaining turned to anger and bitterness. When my husband wouldn't jump through the hoops I created, Maria was there to listen, pick sides, and help fuel my anger."

Maria said things like,

- "If you're not happy, you don't have to stay with him."

- "God doesn't want you to be unhappy."

- "There is a man out there who can make you happy. You just have to go find him."

Although Hannah knew God's view on marriage and divorce, she started agreeing with her friend. "I deserved to be happy," she writes.

> When Maria and I would have lunch or drinks, we would point out men we found attractive. It seemed like harmless "girl fun," but thoughts would continue to swirl long after a night out. When the opportunity finally presented itself, I took the first step into what would become a three-year affair. Throughout those three years, Maria was there. She shared her relationship/marriage was the result of an affair, and she was truly happy. I could have this same happiness too. If I expressed angst, she would console me and remind me that as my friend, my happiness was her number-one concern. Many times I felt stuck because she was the only person who knew my darkest secret. Our friendship had become about lies, deception, and secrecy. This "happiness" kept me in bondage, created excruciating pain, and almost cost me my marriage.

Eventually, Hannah saw through Maria's tactics and so-called encouragements. Instead of giving in to Maria's continued advice, she left the affair, repented before her husband, sought counsel, and worked on reconciliation. Hers was a truly happy ending, but the pathway toward it? Excruciating.

WHAT THE BIBLE SAYS

One of the most famous verses about Tempter Trevor comes from 1 Corinthians 15:33: "Don't be fooled by those who say such things, for 'bad company corrupts good character.'" As one who has discipled young women, I can honestly say from experience that the girls who stayed close to Christ chose good friends, and the ones who strayed chose Tempter Trevors. You tend to become whom you hang around with. This is called the chameleon effect. "The chameleon effect refers to non-conscious mimicry of the postures, mannerisms, facial expressions, and other behaviors of one's interaction partners, such that one's behavior passively and unintentionally changes to match that of others in one's current social environment."[2] All that means that we mimic those with whom we spend time. If we hang out with bullies, we tend to become bullies. If we spend all our time with drug addicts, the temptation will be nearly irresistible to delve into drug addiction as well. Like chameleons, we change our colors to fit into the group we most interact with. Proverbs 22:24-25 confirms the chameleon effect: "Don't befriend angry people or associate with hot-tempered people, or you will learn to be like them and endanger your soul."

So does this mean that we can never befriend someone with bad behavior? Not according to Paul in 1 Corinthians 5:9-11. He begins: "When I wrote to you before, I told you not to associate with people who indulge in sexual sin. But I wasn't talking about unbelievers who indulge in sexual sin, or are greedy, or cheat people, or worship idols. You would have to leave this world to avoid people like that." Of course we interact with those outside the faith. The Great Commission commands this kind of generous friendship. Jesus left the 99 for the one, and his longing is that none would perish but that all would come to know him—and he graciously includes us in the story of evangelism. But look how Paul warns us about the people we spend the most time with in his next breath: "I meant that you are not to associate with anyone who claims to be a believer yet indulges in sexual sin, or is greedy, or worships idols, or is abusive, or is a drunkard, or cheats people. Don't even eat with such people."

Chances are your Tempter Trevor didn't present himself as a rebel upon first look. Instead, he fit in with you and your beliefs, which helped you feel safe in pursuing him. It was only later that you understood his outward appearance didn't match his inward beliefs, and by the time you figured it out, he had you hooked. Paul warns us not to even associate with or share a table with him.

Remember that Satan is known as the Tempter. In the wilderness, he exemplified the worst of deadly friends, a tempter extraordinaire. His tactics are instructive. Let's read about his interaction with Jesus in Matthew 4:3-10:

> During that time the devil came and said to him, "If you are the Son of God, tell these stones to become loaves of bread."

> But Jesus told him, "No! The Scriptures say,

> 'People do not live by bread alone, but by every word that comes from the mouth of God.'"

> Then the devil took him to the holy city, Jerusalem, to the highest point of the Temple, and said, "If you are the Son of God, jump off! For the Scriptures say,

> 'He will order his angels to protect you.
> And they will hold you up with their hands
> so you won't even hurt your foot on a stone.'"

> Jesus responded, "The Scriptures also say, 'You must not test the LORD your God.'"

> Next the devil took him to the peak of a very high mountain and showed him all the kingdoms of the world and their glory. "I will give it all to you," he said, "If you will kneel down and worship me."

"Get out of here, Satan," Jesus told him. "For the Scriptures say,

'You must worship the LORD YOUR GOD
and serve only him.'"

Satan always starts tempting others by saying half truths about God. He plants seeds of doubt about God's goodness and verity with the word *if*. He used similar tactics with Eve in the Garden of Eden when he asked her, "The serpent was the shrewdest of all the wild animals the LORD God had made. One day he asked the woman, 'Did God really say you must not eat the fruit from any of the trees in the garden?'" (Genesis 3:1). Not only did he begin with trying to instill doubt, but in both cases he swiftly followed up with an enticement toward ungodly action. In Jesus's case, he would make bread from stones in direct obedience to Satan, and in Eve's case, she would eat forbidden fruit. The theoretical temptation ended in a concrete disobedience. And this is how Tempter Trevor works. He empowers you to question the goodness and reality of God, and soon after he presents a temptation of action.

You see this same dynamic in all three temptations. The first two: If you are this, then do this foolish thing. (Lie/doubt, action.) The last one: I own it all; worship me. (Lie, action.) This pattern of behavior is important to discern if you're going to gain victory from a Tempter Trevor.

A truly deadly friendship involves deception and coercion toward sin. Note how Jesus dealt with all three temptations. He recited Scripture back to the Tempter. (But be wary of someone who quotes Scripture to you, then twists it, as Satan did here.) While it may be hard to discern Tempter Trevor's intentions initially, knowing the Bible and its wisdom will empower you to see through his tactics.

The oft-memorized verse in 1 Corinthians 10:13 is helpful as well:

"The temptations in your life are no different from what others experience. And God is faithful. He will not allow the temptation to be more than you can stand. When you are tempted, he will show you a way out so that you can endure." Not only will knowing and reciting biblical truth to a tempting friend be beneficial, but also actively looking for a way of escape—knowing God has already provided one—will help you flee. In the case of Tempter Trevor, that way of escape is often a complete separation from him.

Tempter Trevor will lead you where you don't want to go. In your rational state, you may say to yourself that you'd like to obey God and live a life that makes him smile, but in the moment with your tempting friend, you suddenly become the person you know you don't want to be.

> Violent people mislead their companions, leading them down a harmful path (Proverbs 16:29).

> They are the worst kind of rebel, full of slander. They are as hard as bronze and iron, and they lead others into corruption (Jeremiah 6:28).

If you find yourself on the yo-yo of desire, longing to be pure apart from the person but plunging headlong into sin when you're with him or her, it's time to reevaluate. Remember that love is not about twisting you to be your worst. Love wants what is best for you. It rejoices with righteousness. "It does not rejoice about injustice but rejoices whenever the truth wins out," Paul writes in 1 Corinthians 13:6. If your friend causes you to do unjust things to yourself or others, and if Tempter Trevor twists truth, coercing you to believe lies about God, he does not love you well. He is using you.

Psalm 26:4-5 is instructive in this case: "I do not spend time with liars or go along with hypocrites. I hate the gatherings of those who do evil, and I refuse to join in with the wicked." The psalmist simply tells us to refrain from spending time with people who corrupt us. We make a choice not to join in. But the opposite is also true. If we replace who we spend our time with and choose good, safe, empowering people rather than tempters, the result is *not* that we will stagnate, but that we will actually grow in a positive direction. "Walk with the wise and become wise; associate with fools and get in trouble" (Proverbs 13:20). Psalm 1 further reinforces this notion, but takes it one step further: delighting in the law of the Lord.

> Oh, the joys of those who do not follow the advice of the wicked, or stand around with sinners, or join in with mockers. But they delight in the law of the Lord, meditating on it day and night. They are like trees planted along the riverbank, bearing fruit each season. Their leaves never wither, and they prosper in all they do. But not the wicked! They are like worthless chaff, scattered by the wind. They will be condemned at the time of judgment. Sinners will have no place among the godly. For the Lord watches over the path of the godly, but the path of the wicked leads to destruction.

Essentially, the psalmist's advice is this: We choose good friends, know the truth by reading the Word of God, and we avoid spending time with those who would corrupt us.

But what if Tempter Trevor is part of your group of friends? Then things become tricky. If you leave him, you jeopardize your position in the group. In that case, it's time to evaluate if your friend group is full of a bunch of Tempter Trevors, or if he is the sole one. If he is, then perhaps have a conversation with the group of friends (with Trevor in attendance) to address his destructive behavior—a sort of intervention.

Of course, this type of honest work doesn't always turn out well. Most people are afraid of confrontation like this because it threatens to upset the entire balance of friendship. As writer Carlin Flora puts it,

> As much as we need to take responsibility for being better friends and for our part in relationship conflict and break-ups, quite a few factors surrounding friendship are out of our control. Social network embeddedness, where you and another person have many friends in common, for instance, is a big challenge. Let's say someone crosses a line, but you don't want to disturb the group, so you don't declare that you no longer think of him as a friend. You pull back from him, but not so much that it will spark a direct confrontation, whereby people would then be forced to invite only one of you, but not both, to events. Sometimes we are yoked to bad friends.[3]

The awkwardness of confrontation makes this a difficult situation.

AM I TEMPTER TREVOR?

If you feel far from God, and you're building into relationships that applaud your sinful choices, you may be part of a peer group that's not ideal. If someone tells you that she needs to separate from you because she's not her best self around you, it is time to introspect and see if you've become Tempter Trevor. Causing someone else to violate his or her conscience is wrong. Jesus had strong words for those who cause or empower his children to sin. "If you cause one of these little ones who trusts in me to fall into sin, it would be better for you to have a large millstone tied around your neck and be drowned in the depths of the sea" (Matthew 18:6). If this is your case, find a close friend who loves Jesus and confess your sin and ask for prayer. You cannot heal from this in isolation; you need wholesome community that dares to hold you accountable and tell you the truth.

Tempter Trevor usually runs in packs, and those groups don't always entice you to sin in "big sin" ways. You may have a peer group that bends toward materialism or one-upmanship in possessions or abilities. You may find yourself drinking more around a particular group of friends.

Remember that you become who you most hang out with. It's never easy to make a break with friends you love deeply who influence you away from Jesus, but be assured that those who leave friend groups for his sake will find a greater treasure eventually.

And remember this: Sometimes those who tempt you to do wrong are members of your family. Jesus reminded us that his primary allegiance to the Father trumped even his family. When they came looking for him, he simply asked, "Who is my mother? Who are my brothers?" (Matthew 12:48). He later reminded the disciples that the most important relationship we have, even among our family members, is him. "Everyone who has given up houses or brothers or sisters or father or mother or children or property, for my sake, will receive a hundred times as much in return and will inherit eternal life" (Matthew 19:29).

FAKER FIONA

"A False Witness Who Pours Out Lies"

aker Fiona thrives today, and her fuel is often the skewed platform of social media.

I met one online I'll call Zoe. She presented herself as a very put-together follower of Christ. Her website and online presence certainly highlighted this. And initially when I met her, I saw no red flags. She exuded WYSIWYG (what you see is what you get). But one day, she sent me a picture of herself with a supposed new hairstyle. I could tell she had inserted her face into this hairstyle, so I wrote something back like, "Oh, you're trying to see what new style you want. I like it!"

To which Zoe responded, with incredulity, that, no, that actually was her, and she did have that hairstyle. It was, she said, a photo of her right now with that hair.

I didn't push back, though I could clearly see the telltale signs of photoshopping. Instead, I backtracked through our friendship, particularly what she shared on social media, and put on my investigator hat. I found other pictures, clearly altered, that validated her extraordinary stories, making everything she had shared suspect. I soon realized that her online life was almost entirely manufactured, and that her heartfelt conversations with me were nearly all laced with lies.

I thought back to an encounter I had with her early in our friendship. She unfolded a fantastic story, one that roped me in, telling me about how she'd been in line at a store, and the person behind her started harassing her, almost violently. Everyone in the store watched, as she continued to banter with her new nemesis behind her. As Zoe recounted the story, she stood to her feet and pantomimed the interchange—it was very animated. I remember leaning forward, wanting to know what happened next. "So what did you say to her?" I asked. I couldn't imagine a more awkward grocery store story!

She stopped, looked me square in the eyes, and said without emotion, "I just made that entire story up." I should have walked away from the friendship then.

Another friend, Caroline, had no ill intent in having an untrustworthy bent. She simply spent her life overresponding to people in her life. Longing to meet every single need she saw, she neglected to be truthful in conversations with me. Instead of saying, "No, I can't do that," or "No, I'll need to pass" to an invitation, she tried to convince me that she had, in fact, attended a mutual function. Except that she hadn't. When my confusion surfaced, she shape-shifted before my eyes, and she spent a great deal of energy defending herself. Yes, she had attended. Yes, she was there. How dare I say otherwise? After our halted interaction, I realized I couldn't trust her yes or her no, and I backed away from the friendship.

Faker Fiona is often amazing—your closest friend that you've shared everything with. She is 100 percent with you. Until she is not. She moves from gregariously loving you with fervor to absolutely hating you with the same passion. Often you don't know what you did to cause the shift.

These friends are also deceptive, appearing to be one way but acting another, and when the friend breakup occurs, they take your personal information and spread it far and wide.

Another aspect of her personality is fear. She may not be malicious (like Caroline above), but she cannot be trusted. She worries constantly about what other people think of her, so she overcommits, then finds herself lying to cover herself. Her speech is peppered with half truths, and, when pressed, she subtly or not so subtly shifts the blame from herself to you. She is a false witness—meaning you cannot trust what she says because often what she says is not backed up by her actions.

Unfortunately, our world of social media gives Faker Fiona a beautiful stage to thrive on. Folks can construct their external lives in a way that makes them look enviable, when in reality, they don't live up to their own personal hype. Like virtual reality, we can create our realities with a click of a mouse or a snap of an Instagram filter. (Even the filters make us look better!) Not only that, the very nature of this kind of artificial connection undermines our relationships.

Chamath Palihapitiya, the former vice president for user growth at Facebook, said this: "The short-term, dopamine-driven feedback loops that we have created are destroying how society works. No civil discourse, no cooperation, misinformation, mistruth."[1] Without face-to-face communication, Faker Fiona pulls off all sorts of shenanigans, masquerading as one thing when her actual life pales in comparison.

TRAITS

Faker Fiona behaves this way:

- She creates a persona of her perfect life online, but her off-line life does not positively compare to it.

- She is untrustworthy; you cannot believe what she says.

- She becomes two different people—Public Fiona and Private Fiona.

- She pathologically lies, meaning there's no real reason for the lie. It seems to be her native language. She has a "long history (maybe lifelong history) of frequent and repeated lying for which no apparent psychological motive or external benefit can be discerned."[2]

- Often combined with narcissistic traits, she lies about her achievements, embellishing her accomplishments. She might have attended a lecture at Cambridge, but then she tells everyone she was a visiting professor.

- She seems oblivious to the fact that other people may actually fact-check her life.

- Likewise, she doesn't seem to fear being outed.

- She says things to appease you when you bring up discrepancies. And for a while, those excuses work.

- She easily morphs into the crowd she's currently in. If she's in a group of intellectuals, she becomes a brainiac. If she's hanging out with fashionistas, she talks about the latest runway crazes.

- She's excessively good about stroking your ego. She gives a lot of compliments, almost blushingly so.

- She may promise to change her ways, but that promise is short lived.

- She makes grandiose promises, but does not keep them. She flakes out regularly.

- Instead of actually being a good person, she spends an inordinate amount of time pretending to be one.
- She talks behind your back.
- She takes advantage of people who are trusting and caring.
- She is often a hypochondriac.
- All stories involving relationships have a villain, and that villain is never her. She's the victim.
- Her stories feature her as the hero (on a grand scale) or her as the victim (in an almost impossibly sad way).
- When confronted, she resorts to bullying.
- She has Dr. Jekyll and Mr. Hyde tendencies—sweet when you believe her carefully constructive narrative, wolflike when you don't.
- When discovered, Faker Fiona doesn't seem to be bothered by your pain. She doesn't care that she lied, and has no earthly idea why it would have bothered you.
- She also, if backed into a corner, will retaliate fiercely, blaming you. You leave the conversation feeling like you did something wrong, even though you were bringing up her own proven lie.
- She only has online friends. In real life, she's isolated. (You may be her only real-life friend.)
- She tells engaging but impossible stories.
- She triangulates, pitting one friend or family member against another. This removes suspicion from her own antics and lies.

- She changes her stories (often completely) to fit whatever audience she has.

- She has gotten away with her behavior and seems impervious to recourse.

- She is not self-aware.

- She shows no emotion when she lies. She can deadpan her lies, making them virtually undetectable, and, contrary to popular belief, she can look you in the eyes when she lies.

- Often her lies help her reputation. Beneath the lies is a deep insecurity of wanting to be popular and noticed, so she embellishes.

- She cycles through friendships fairly rapidly.

- And when a friendship ends, it truly ends—badly and with a lot of negative fanfare. She'll curry favor with you by denigrating the former friend.

- She is prone to exaggeration. A cough becomes pneumonia. A parking ticket becomes a run-in with the police. (In this way, she resembles Dramatic Drake).

- She tells other people's stories as if they were her own, and she is entirely convincing (as in the case of the pastor who stole sermons in the Narcissist Nolan chapter).

- She dodges direct questions. Instead of answering, she shoots a question back at you.

- She knows her audience. If you won't believe her tall tales about health, she'll avoid telling you those and reserve them for another friend who will. She constantly tests how you respond to her exaggerations. If she suspects you are suspicious, she retreats.

- She has reinvented herself many times.

- She nearly always has the last word in a conversation.

- She has had many jobs over her lifetime, moving from job to job.

- She has a history of unstable relationships, often estranged, including family members.

- Someone has warned you about her lying.

- She is relaxed when she lies.

- Her smile bothers you; it seems fake, not genuine.

- She says one thing, but acts in the opposite way. She may appear to be a health nut, but you may just discover fast-food trash in her car.

- She may have told an entirely different origin story. For instance, she may share that she grew up in poverty, when you know she had a middle-class upbringing.

- You get the sense that she believes her lies as if they are true.

- She exaggerates any sort of accolade.

- Time often exposes her lies. She thrives in short conversations and quick spurts of interaction, but over the long haul, cracks appear. This is why she seems to flit from one friend group to another.

- She seems to get a "high" when she lies.

INTERACTIONS WITH FAKER FIONA

Kayley ran into a counterfeit when she was stationed in Hawaii and her husband, Justin, was deployed. She writes, "I made a male friend, Frank, at work who I felt pretty confident was gay. We mostly hung out at work or in groups, but started doing a few things together just the two of us—pedicures, baking cookies, etc."

One day she told Frank, "I don't want to hang out with you one-on-one because it makes my husband uncomfortable for me to hang out with a guy he doesn't know." In that moment, Frank turned into a whole different person. She writes, "He called Justin ugly names for telling me who I could and couldn't hang out with (and for the record, we still could have hung out at work and in a group). He tried to tell me I deserved someone better." It turned out he wasn't gay; it was an elaborate ruse he used to get close to Kayley.

She ended the friendship. "Ultimately, I told him if he was asking me to choose between being his friend and honoring my husband, I choose my husband every time."

Patricia occasionally worked for Ally. On one particular straw-that-broke-the-friendship's-back event, Ally accused Patricia of being slothful when, in reality, Ally had given her permission to take time off. "She didn't have my back," Patricia said. "When the manager saw me leave an hour early, he called Ally. And instead of her reassuring the manager that she'd given me permission to leave early, she called me immediately and reprimanded me. I realized I never would have called her out on something like that. I trusted her and her judgment. When it dawned on me that she didn't, I could see that our friendship was one-sided." They had a talk for closure, but their relationship never recovered. When Patricia didn't fuel Ally's drama, it ceased to exist. Abigail Van Buren is fond of asking readers who undergo such drama with relationships to ask themselves if they're better off without the other person in their lives. In Patricia's case, the answer was a resounding yes.

Erin shares about a friendship that she thought was one way, but it ended up being completely the opposite. "I e-mailed a friend, Margo, who had moved away and I had lost contact with. I was struggling with relationships with other people we both knew and hoped she would have insight that would help me understand what was going on. The first e-mails were cordial, but by the end of the exchange she lectured me on my bitterness and unforgiveness, gave me a numbered lists of my sins, quoted 'faithful are the wounds of a friend,' and claimed to be correcting me because she loved me."

This hurt Erin, but she realized Margo was wrong about her accusations, reasoning, *How could she know me better than I knew myself?* Still, Erin held onto the e-mail correspondence, even though friends have told her to get rid of it. "Once I'd reached a place of strength, I could read it and see much more clearly the abuse in her words. It's given me the ability to recognize phrases that I don't have to believe when I hear them. I even found strength in my responses to her because I disagreed with her conclusions and presented my own view with relatively few cheap shots." She adds some wise advice for us all: "At this point in my life, it's not about branding this person as bad, but of recognizing unacceptable behavior and choosing not to get too close to anyone who displays that kind of behavior."

Layla shares about something less insidious, but probably more common—groups of women at church:

> I sat in numerous church groups with ladies claiming to
> be so friendly. In and around other women they'd smile,
> laugh, and all would go to lunch after weekly Bible study
> meetings. But when it came to smaller groups or trying to
> have one-on-one interaction with these ladies, they would
> act like junior high girls playing games of favorites and

spending more time with those who could make them look good. [They weren't interested in] a genuine relationship.

This kind of interaction left Layla feeling alone. She coped by reminding herself of the truth. "It was extremely difficult, and I felt very left out and alone until I realized how many of them just wanted superficial relationships."

Jules was new in her church where her husband became an associate pastor. Initially, the senior pastor's wife, Kendra, exuded kindness and inclusivity. "She was very welcoming at first and invited me often to do things. Kendra is very open and loves to host parties and have people in her home. She talks easily about her family and shares openly some of her experiences in life. I thought this was going to be a new friendship, and it ended up being very painful."

Kendra initially invited Jules to serve in the church, but instead, she often planned events without her, seldom communicating what was going on or when events would happen. "She asked me once to be the host for a Valentine's Day party, but only if I did things her way. I tried sharing with her several ideas to accommodate her wishes, but in the end, she said I needed to be flexible."

Jules has had to find her own ways to serve without relying on Kendra's invitation. "I now build relationships with other people I am more comfortable with," she writes, "people who seem more genuine and less focused on external things like having the best home, the best family, talking about oneself too much, and organizing parties. That's her vision of women's ministry."

WHAT THE BIBLE SAYS

Identifying Faker Fiona isn't easy. Because she is adept at deception, she's spent her life perfecting her technique. Still, she cannot maintain an illusion forever. In the context of community, her cracks will appear. There will be discrepancies, excuses, and things that don't add up.

Folks like her are so persuasive; they can convince you of nearly everything. Job reminds us, "These men say that night is day; they claim that the darkness is light" (Job 17:12). Like Tempter Trevor, her behaviors pattern that of the master liar, Satan himself. Remember, lying is the air he breathes; it's his native language, his constant fallback.

We need to be careful not to demonize Faker Fiona, realizing that her patterns of behavior have been learned (and sometimes practiced) over a lifetime. Understanding where her lying comes from is instructive. The problem comes when we internalize her lies as truth. When we do, we enable her lies, and when we enable her lies, we allow her to both thrive *and* deceive more people.

Jesus had some pointed words about the Pharisees who had boastful words, but whose lives didn't back up their claims. Jesus equates the Pharisees, people prone to religious fakery, to children of the devil. He said, "For you are the children of your father the devil, and you love to do the evil things he does. He was a murderer from the beginning. He has always hated the truth, because there is no truth in him. When he lies, it is consistent with his character; for he is a liar and the father of lies" (John 8:44). It's important to remember that his ire was aimed at people within a religious system who oppressed others. Your response to Faker Fiona won't be as pointed, unless she is actively seeking to harm others with her lies and alternate stories. Still, it's good to see how seriously Jesus takes deceptive people. Read what he says in Matthew 23:1-7,25-28:

> The teachers of religious law and the Pharisees are the
> official interpreters of the law of Moses. So practice and

obey whatever they tell you, but don't follow their example. For they don't practice what they teach. They crush people with unbearable religious demands and never lift a finger to ease the burden. Everything they do is for show. On their arms they wear extra wide prayer boxes with Scripture verses inside, and they wear robes with extra long tassels. And they love to sit at the head table at banquets and in the seats of honor in the synagogues. They love to receive respectful greetings as they walk in the marketplaces, and to be called "Rabbi"...What sorrow awaits you teachers of religious law and you Pharisees. Hypocrites! For you are so careful to clean the outside of the cup and the dish, but inside you are filthy—full of greed and self-indulgence! You blind Pharisee! First wash the inside of the cup and the dish, and then the outside will become clean, too. What sorrow awaits you teachers of religious law and you Pharisees. Hypocrites! For you are like whitewashed tombs—beautiful on the outside but filled on the inside with dead people's bones and all sorts of impurity. Outwardly you look like righteous people, but inwardly your hearts are filled with hypocrisy and lawlessness.

Look at the list of Faker Fiona's traits, and you'll see the same tendencies in the Pharisees of Jesus's age. Faker Fiona doesn't practice what she preaches. Everything she does is for show, as if she's acting on a grand stage for the accolades of others. She loves praise and acclaim, the best seats, the highest honors. She appears one way, but inwardly she believes and behaves the opposite. Jesus warns us that folks like this are like grave markers painted white, pretty on the outside, full of death inside. The greatest marker of Faker Fiona is hypocrisy.

Paul warns us about folks like this, particularly those within the church who actively lead others astray. He writes, "These people are false apostles. They are deceitful workers who disguise themselves as apostles of Christ. But I am not surprised! Even Satan disguises himself as an angel of light. So it is no wonder that his servants also disguise themselves as servants of righteousness. In the end they will get the punishment their wicked deeds deserve" (2 Corinthians 11:13-15). Again we see this correlation with the Evil One and a faker. Deception is the handiwork of Satan, and when others are actively involved in deception, they unremittingly do his work. When there is deception, destruction results—in broken hearts, a church's damaged reputation, and cynicism on behalf of the one who's been duped.

What are we to do with Faker Fiona? The first task is to discern what she's done and to uncover her possible reasons for fakery, if that's even possible. But that's not always easy to do. Jeremiah 17:9 reminds us, "The human heart is the most deceitful of all things, and desperately wicked. Who really knows how bad it is?" How we deal with her depends on the level of deception, the maliciousness of her actions, and whether she seems open to hearing constructive criticism. If she is a very close friend, and you want to continue the relationship, speaking the truth to her is the first step. As I've mentioned before, Paul reminds us in Ephesians 4:15 that doing this ensures and empowers our own spiritual growth: "Instead, we will speak the truth in love, growing in every way more and more like Christ, who is the head of his body, the church." This is what mature believers do in community; they love people enough to kindly call them out.

Faker Fiona's reaction will guide what you do next. If she receives the loving rebuke, you can begin the arduous process of helping her live a life that exemplifies trustworthiness, while you cautiously extend grace. (Remember, trust is not granted automatically. It is earned over time based on reliable, trustworthy behavior.) We see this kind of interaction in 2 Corinthians 2, when Paul recounts how he wrote a pointed letter about a man caught in egregious sin. His approach was not that of triumphal excitement but of pain mixed with a shepherd's love. He writes, "I wrote that letter in great anguish, with a troubled heart and many tears. I didn't want to grieve you, but I wanted to let you know how much love I have for you" (2:4). His confrontation bore the marks of deep-seated love. And, apparently, the man changed his ways and repented.

Paul's next instruction helps us as we restore Faker Fiona: "Now, however, it is time to forgive and comfort him. Otherwise he may be overcome by discouragement. So I urge you now to reaffirm your love for him" (2:7-8).

Of course, not all Faker Fionas respond well when called out. Proverbs 17:12 warns, "It is safer to meet a bear robbed of her cubs than to confront a fool caught in foolishness." If she retaliates forcefully when you bring up a discrepancy in her life, you will have better intel, knowing what to do next. Depending on how the Lord leads you, you could walk through Matthew 18:15-17. (See chapter 2 about Unreliable Uma for a more detailed discussion.) If she doesn't respond, bring a few more who also discern her fake ways. Still not "hearing" you? The next step is to bring her to the leaders of the church.

But more likely, if Faker Fiona continues her destructive patterns, it will be time to separate from her. The psalmist writes, "I do not spend time with liars or go along with hypocrites" (Psalm 26:4). By continuing in the relationship, you empower and validate her lies. In a way, you're giving Faker Fiona permission to continue deceiving others. The typical pattern for Faker Fiona is this: She cycles through many, many friends. Chances are, you're one of them, and it's better to make a clean break. If she happens to be a member of your family, separating permanently may not be an option. In that case, erecting good boundaries will help mitigate her abuse. This may include always calling her out on false stories, walking away when she's lying, or separating for a period of time.

AM I FAKER FIONA?

People who live a life of lies have a hard time discerning whether they are lying. Often they convince themselves that their stories are true. That you're worried you might be her is a strong indication that you're not. People who introspect and wonder if they're hurting others are usually not hurting others; instead, they are hard on themselves.

If you are Faker Fiona, somewhere along the line someone has confronted you about it. If a friend has accused you of living a fake life, telling lies, or being hypocritical, spend some time journaling through his or her words. On one hand, your friend may be right, and it will be time for you to get on your knees, ask for forgiveness, and begin the arduous process of making amends with those you've lied to. On the other hand, you may have a hyperactive conscience, and the confrontation may be a projection of the confronter's own battle with deceit. This is where having a strong community around you will help. Bring accusations to reliable friends to discern whether there's veracity to their words.

Faker Fiona is a nuisance if she's on the slight spectrum of deception, but if her life is categorized by making up elaborate lies, watch out. In that state, she can be one of the deadliest of friendships, leaving relationship corpses in her wake. Her concern is only for herself, never for her victims, and because of that, she can be dangerous. Caution is advised.

Dramatic Drake

"A Person Who Sows Discord in a Family"

Sasha's e-mails were more like books, without punctuation, excessive in capital letters, always bordering on crisis. For a long time, I engaged, asked questions, prayed a lot. But as I began to tease out her messages and how they lined up with reality, I took a step back. And as I investigated, I realized she seemed to have a need for drama, like she thrived on it. Even if things were small and insignificant incidences, they turned into fiascoes at her fingertips.

Another thing I realized was the difference in her demeanor between her long diatribe correspondences and her somewhat meek appearance in person. I couldn't reconcile the two, but when I discovered many of her words were laced with exaggeration and sometimes even blatant lies, I pulled back from the drama, curious what would happen next. I realized that by listening to and engaging with Sasha on her emergency timetable, I was actually fueling more interaction. When I stopped reacting, she eventually ceased corresponding.

My friend Brandi experienced *my* dramatic ways. It's embarrassing to admit, but if left to my own devices, I become Dramatic

Drake. And often as is the case with him, I can place all my friend-ship eggs in one friendship basket. At the time, I did this with Brandi, giving her everything, pouring out all my angst.

This came on the heels of a move across country when I was incredibly lonely in a new town. My previous friendships from far away suddenly became everything to me, and Brandi received most of my neediness. When she didn't remember my birthday, I pas-sive aggressively wrote about her (not mentioning her name) in a newsletter I composed, detailing my hurt and confusion. I instantly regretted it, particularly when she called me out on it. Finally, I shared why I was hurt, how disappointed I was that she hadn't remembered my birthday, and how let down I felt by her. She gen-tly, but firmly, reminded me that I had made her an idol, that I had poured all my drama into her, expecting her to carry and solve it. She was wearied by it all (and I don't blame her). I've written about this elsewhere, but she said something that stuck with me: "I can't be Jesus to you. Only he can."

Brandi had rightly directed me back to the One who would receive all my drama. I eventually understood that no human is meant to be everything to us, and putting pressure on someone to bear all our hurts (whether big or small, dramatic or mundane) is placing them on the Savior's throne. As a Dramatic Drake, instead of processing my worry and stress with Jesus first, my first reaction was to call Brandi. I learned, instead, to give Jesus the first parts of me, and I asked him to please heal the part of me that was bent toward crying wolf, being dramatic, and demanding that my friends be everything to me. It's too much pressure for them, and it enables me to use others.

I once encountered an online friend, Kathy, who used me as her drama dumping ground. Like Sasha, her e-mails were long and involved, and often included threats of suicide. For several months,

I prayed for her, counseled her, and hoped she wouldn't take her life. I agonized over the idea that if I wasn't there for her, she'd end up making good on her promise and ending her life. I finally had to point her to resources and ask her to find an in-person friend who could walk with her through this difficult season.

In retrospect, I've found that drama often thrives when we aren't in "real-life" friendships with people. We have more leeway to say whatever we want over the veil of e-mail and text than when we're sitting across from a friend. Because many people have been wounded in one-to-one community, they withdraw from real people and instead pursue online friendships. In that space, they feel even freer to share everything that comes to mind. Because there is no genuine back-and-forth like in real life, they tend to overwhelm the other friend, spouting off their fears and worries at all hours of the day and night. That's not to say I didn't try to be there for Kathy, but I realized my help across the miles could not truly benefit her. She needed real-life friends with relational skin in the game.

Dramatic Drake is often dependent on you for his happiness. In fact, he demands that you always be in his life (on his terms) to be happy. He tends toward drama, and calls at all hours of the night with the latest crisis. Oddly, he is suddenly silent when you voice a need. This manifests itself in a one-sided friendship in constant need of rescuing. You can seemingly never satisfy this friend, and his drama only increases each year.

TRAITS

Dramatic Drake behaves this way:

- He repeats the same stories over and over again, and they tend to grow in dramatic effect with each telling.

- When he leaves, you feel utterly drained.
- When you share something little, something that doesn't really bother you, Dramatic Drake jumps on it and tells you it's a huge deal, and you should be really upset.
- Or the opposite occurs—he one-ups your story and tells you how awful his life is in comparison to yours.
- He epitomizes the fairy tale of the boy who cried wolf.
- He actually complains about drama and dramatic people.
- He jumps to ridicule, overreacting easily.
- He is evasive, especially when you investigate one of his elaborate stories.
- Road bumps become mountains to Dramatic Drake.
- Other people recognize and call Dramatic Drake a drama king (or Dramatic Darla a drama queen).
- Others tell him to chill out.
- He is really good at pointing out your weakness as a friend—which is not being there enough for him.
- He works very hard at getting his own way.
- He takes nearly everything personally, even when it's not about him.
- He stirs up drama and seems to delight in doing so.
- He, like Faker Fiona, tends toward hypochondria. (He is convinced he has cancer and often Googles his many symptoms.)
- When you peel back the layers of drama in your group of friends, he is at the midst.

- He is amazing at spinning stories.

- He is deeply connected to his Netflix queue, specific movies, certain actors and actresses. When a series ends, it's the end of his world.

- He loves texting in ALL CAPS.

- He seems to be attractive to drama. He often finds himself in dramatic situations. His choices seem to "ask for it."

- His bad day is the end of the world—even if 90 percent of the day was good and only 10 percent difficult.

- He is critical of others and you. No one lives up to his expectations (they are very high, nearly impossible).

- He seems to be a main character in a soap opera.

- He loves mirrors and tends to obsess over his looks.

- He curries favor and the center of attention.

- He compares himself positively to others (he is better), or negatively (he is the worst).

- He starts interactions with words like, "You'll never believe what so-and-so said!" or similar phraseologies.

- He is picky about what he eats, and is not very fun eating out with. He sends food back.

- He assumes negative intent of you. (You're a friend cheating on him; you're talking about him; you don't have his back.)

- He is a control freak, and if things don't go his way, he overreacts.

- In fact, overreaction is his modus operandi.

- He blows things out of proportion and cannot be talked back down. It's typically escalation that never de-escalates.

- He is paranoid.

- He is vampiric, in that he tends to suck his friends dry.

- He is guilty of catastrophizing the mundane.

- At a party, he has to be the center of attention (or at a restaurant, or at work, or in line).

- He expects you to know him intimately, but often overlooks your needs.

- He can be histrionic, throwing fits for small infractions.

- He has an all-or-nothing mind-set. He cannot see shades of gray. You are either all for him or all against him.

- He has wildly swinging moods.

- He expects you to respond in kind and is deeply disappointed if you react calmly to his latest fiasco.

- He treats you like his personal emergency line.

- He loves the vortex of deepening drama.

- He betrays other people's secrets to you.

- He peppers his speech with the words *never* and *always*. "You are never there for me. You always betray me!"

- He threatens to harm himself if you don't help him to the degree he wants. He has high expectations for how well you rescue, listen, and support him through all his crises.

- He has threatened suicide or has tried it. (Please, even

though Drake is dramatic, take all threats and actions regarding suicide seriously.)

- He easily throws others under the bus.
- His speech is full of hyperbole: "My friend hates my guts!" (after a minor argument).
- He has polarizing political views and believes that people with other opinions are enemies.
- He takes things personally, as an affront.
- He has shared your secrets with others.
- He finds a scapegoat whenever he's found out for doing something wrong.
- He whines. A lot.
- He tends to be obsessive and draws others into his obsessions.
- He gets outraged in a moment.
- He doesn't apologize for his mistakes. Instead, everyone else is at fault.
- He stresses out easily.
- If he has children, he tends to live through his children—pushing his kids to excel in things he lacked or excelled in during his growing-up years.
- He is funny and highly entertaining. He woos a room.
- He freaks out (often) on social media—long, controversial posts that invite more drama in the comments, and then he gets very offended. His posts have comments wars.
- He throws hissy fits over small inconveniences.

- His first world problems read like Third World problems.

- He gossips often.

- He is more concerned about his public reputation than his private actions.

- You leave interaction with him feeling guilty because you disappointed him—again. He is really good at guilt trips.

- He curries grudges, and nothing you say or do can dissuade him to forgive and move on.

- He also lures you into gossip.

- Your other friends absolutely do not like Dramatic Drake.

ENCOUNTERS WITH DRAMATIC DRAKE

Elia has two overly dramatic friends.

> One is a fellow homeschool mom. I should have known there was something wrong when she said she didn't have female friends her entire life. She plays coy and truly thinks she's not the center of the world person, but she is way off. In reality, she makes everything all about her. She also is very resentful when people back away from her, yet not from me. She has actually said to me, "I don't know why I get left behind. Why don't friends walk away from you too?"

Elia's other friend "uses social media to share things that my gut instinct tells me is just to incite people. She seems to revel in the drama and stirring up of things, but then she claims hurt feelings when people fight back or call her out." Looking back on both friendships, Elia wrote these wise words: "In both friendships, I see a false belief of reality and understanding of how people view them."

Callie had a friend in college, Hayley, who drained her, though she couldn't put her finger on why. Except that every time she left an interaction with her, she felt utterly spent and had zero desire to spend time with Hayley again. Everything grew into histrionic proportions. A missed test became the end of her school career; an argument seemed to morph into utter despair and rejection; a lost pair of shoes tipped her toward crying fits. One weekend, things reached a culmination. In a series of lengthy and depression-heavy texts, Hayley threatened to cut herself, then kill herself, in the quiet of her room. Her words were so convincing, Callie panicked. She connected in person with Hayley and made her promise not to kill herself. Turns out, Hayley hadn't been serious. Her demeanor in person didn't match the tone of her texts. Callie then sought counsel from others on how to best respond to Hayley in the future, though after that encounter, Callie did pull away.

Franklin has a sister, Emma, whose heart bleeds for the world. "My younger sister has a big heart—big enough for her to hold all the problems of everyone she's ever met or cares to meet. But it also means her world revolves around everyone's issue," he writes.

> What that meant for me growing up was a never-ending game of guesses. I could never know whether or not my words or actions would set her off. Did I say something negative about a politician? Once she chewed me out for questioning the current president's policy decisions because "I don't know his heart." Did I criticize one of her friends who was picking on her? "How could [I] be so mean to [her] friend?" No matter what I did, my sister

took offense on behalf of anyone and everyone—only her version of the world mattered.

Franklin would pay the consequences if he disagreed with her view of the world.

> I grew up walking on eggshells covering land mines. Sometimes we had a great relationship. Other times I crunched on the wrong shell, and everything blew up. You would think reaching adulthood would mitigate some of the drama, but to this day, my sister's version of the world simply cannot be contradicted. Family conversations are an exercise in kung-fu-like maneuvering around potentially explosive topics. Any depth of friendship is impossible without the ability to simply disagree.

What the Bible Says

Thankfully, we're not without guidance when it comes to dealing with Dramatic Drake. Several verses highlight some of his traits. In Galatians 5:15, we're all warned about the dangers of picking on and picking at others: "If you are always biting and devouring one another, watch out! Beware of destroying one another." If we engage in similar behavior, stooping to the level of someone prone to drama, we may end up hurting more than ourselves. Our places of worship may suffer too—made clear by Paul when he addresses the problems in several congregations.

A few verses later, Paul writes about the results of living a sin-infused life. Note the harsh language:

> When you follow the desires of your sinful nature, the results are very clear: sexual immorality, impurity, lustful pleasures, idolatry, sorcery, hostility, quarreling, jealousy, outbursts of anger, selfish ambition, dissension, division,

envy, drunkenness, wild parties, and other sins like these. Let me tell you again, as I have before, that anyone living that sort of life will not inherit the Kingdom of God.

Lumped in with sexual immorality and sorcery are words like *quarreling, jealousy, outbursts,* and *dissension.* Not that all dramatic folks exhibit these traits, but it is telling.

When a dramatic person jumps over the line from personal drama to involving other people, she begins tearing at the fabric of her faith community. In Titus 3:10-11, Paul advises, "If people are causing divisions among you, give a first and second warning. After that, have nothing more to do with them. For people like that have turned away from the truth, and their own sins condemn them." He takes very seriously people who sow discord. Paul's advice is to confront, then walk away. He further iterates, "Again I say, don't get involved in foolish, ignorant arguments that only start fights" (2 Timothy 2:23). This New Testament wisdom is backed up with Old Testament admonishment: "A troublemaker plants seeds of strife; gossip separates the best of friends" (Proverbs 16:28).

Jesus warns about people whose lives revolve around them, who seem to need to be at the center of attention, particularly in religious circles. "When you pray, don't be like the hypocrites who love to pray publicly on street corners and in the synagogues where everyone can see them. I tell you the truth, that is all the reward they will ever get" (Matthew 6:5). It may seem easy to gloss over these verses and take ourselves or our dramatic friends out of them. After all, we're not necessarily praying on corners or currying attention in church. But in the internet age, where everybody can have 15 minutes of fame, "Everyone can see them." We now have a worldwide stage, a place where drama is praised, clicked through, and applauded. You may not have a dramatic friend in real life, but chances are you know one online.

So what do we do when we encounter Dramatic Drake? A lot depends on the harm factor. Is he willfully enacting harm on others? Or is he broken and simply trying to make up for an insecure nature? If Dramatic Drake listens to your concerns and actively strives to change, that's a beautiful welcome mat to continue in the relationship. However, if he continues to exhibit a pattern of behavior that shows little or no regard for his actions, you may need to redefine the friendship and enact strong boundaries around it. Some of the best wisdom comes from Proverbs 26:17-26.

> Interfering in someone else's argument
> is as foolish as yanking a dog's ears.
>
> Just as damaging
> as a madman shooting a deadly weapon
> is someone who lies to a friend
> and then says, "I was only joking."
>
> Fire goes out without wood,
> and quarrels disappear when gossip stops.
> A quarrelsome person starts fights
> as easily as hot embers light charcoal or fire lights wood.
>
> Rumors are dainty morsels
> that sink deep into one's heart.
>
> Smooth words may hide a wicked heart,
> just as a pretty glaze covers a clay pot.
>
> People may cover their hatred with pleasant words,
> but they're deceiving you.
> They pretend to be kind, but don't believe them.
> Their hearts are full of many evils.
> While their hatred may be concealed by trickery,
> their wrongdoing will be exposed in public.

Let's unpack these verses.

- Sometimes dramatic people try to draw you into someone else's drama, and that never ends well. Interfering is like pulling on a dangerous dog's ears. Do it at your own peril. Remember, you've only heard one person's (dramatic) side of the story. Rushing in with prejudgment (instead of cautiously questioning or choosing not to involve yourself at all) will put the third party on the defensive.

- If your dramatic friend says inflammatory things, then berates you for taking her seriously ("I was only joking."), it's time to reevaluate the friendship.

- When you notice your friend talking about others in a gossipy way, the best thing to do is say nothing. Or leave the conversation. Fewer words and less engagement equals less drama. If you add words and let yourself get riled up, you will reap more drama.

- Remember the nature of knowing insider information. It's like a drug. It makes you feel both superior and special. But what if those rumors are false? And even if they are true, you didn't experience them firsthand, and there is most likely a slant to the story you know nothing about.

- Some dramatic people are extremely articulate. They are hard to pin down, and when you confront them, you often feel like you're crazy. (On the outside they appear normal, and you feel like you've made a mistake in confronting them. Remember, Jesus says a tree is known by its fruit, not merely by its bark.)

- Some folks prone to drama mask their words with

pretend kindness, which makes teasing out their intentions extremely difficult.

- If you feel like someone is pretending to get attention, then they most likely are. Trust your gut.

- Actions. Always look at actions.

But what if you're caught in the maelstrom of Dramatic Drake's words, and you can't seem to extricate yourself? How do you live? Especially if you're bombarded with negative information about others, or the escalation of overreaction in your friend? Paul reminds us to reorient our thinking by fixing our thoughts on truth. He writes in Philippians 4:8, "Fix your thoughts on what is true, and honorable, and right, and pure, and lovely, and admirable. Think about things that are excellent and worthy of praise."

When I've been in my dramatic states, friends who look beyond my spiraling downward are quick (and kind) to remind me of what is good in my life. They tell me the truth. This world is not all about me, nor am I just about to slip off the precipice of sadness. They help me see the blessings in the mess, the beauty underlying the mayhem. And when I have a dramatic friend, I can also offer this same perspective. Another problem is that if I spend too much time with a dramatic person bent toward negativity, his cynicism and pessimism rub off on me. That's when remembering the truth of Philippians 4:8 helps reorient me toward the good things God is still doing in this broken world.

A Caution

Not all people caught in drama (or narcissism or predatory behavior) are doing this of their own volition. It's important to leave room for the possibility of mental illness. Dramatic Drake may be battling diagnosed or undiagnosed bipolar disorder. If you suspect any of your friends are living with a mental illness, consult a licensed counselor. Be sure to pray and tread lightly around the subject, but do be truthful with what you're observing. You may end up helping your friend get the psychological and medical help he needs.

AM I DRAMATIC DRAKE?

As I mentioned at the beginning of this chapter, I was (and sometimes still am) Dramatic Drake. Of all the deadly friendships, this one is my Achilles' heel. Yes, people have told me I'm dramatic, and yes, I've looked seriously at this trait in myself. Perhaps the best way to determine if you bend toward the dramatic is simply asking several of your friends if they see you this way. Thankfully, over the past several years, my closest friends have noticed growth. Because of their kind confrontation and my desire to change, married with God's beautiful ability to change a life, I am choosing to take a deep breath before I jump into drama. I've often caught myself before I've started down the road of hypochondria. Since I am a wordsmith, I've had to reevaluate the way I use words. I know I have the ability to write or tell a story that places me at the center (whether as victim or hero). I am not proud of this part of me, and I sincerely long for continued transformation.

Another way you can discern if you're Dramatic Drake is if you cycle through a lot of relationships, particularly if you had big blow-ups at the end of your past friendships. Be cautious of thinking a friend breakup is only about the other person's behavior. You actually may be the common denominator.

Dramatic Drake, as I mentioned before, is handled differently depending on his degree of drama and how much he leaves others in pain in his drama wake. Seek out a wise friend who can help you discern just how broken Dramatic Drake is, and what the best way to proceed may be. You may need to separate for a time, then test the relationship hesitantly when you reenter it. Or you may need to wave goodbye.

Part Two

How to Find Health

JOSEPH

*They bruised his feet with fetters and placed his neck
in an iron collar. Until the time came to fulfill his
dreams, the LORD tested Joseph's character.*

GENESIS 40:18-19

Not long after I met Jesus at 15, I learned about Joseph. His story captivated me. As a girl, I had experienced my own sense of betrayal by others, along with abuse and neglect. Joseph's ability to endure struck me then, and it strikes admiration in me today. Joseph not only experienced deadly friendships (Potiphar, Potiphar's wife, the cupbearer, the baker), but much of his anguish came at the hands of people who were supposed to love him well. Betrayed by his brothers, nearly killed, then trafficked to slave owners, he had every right to be bitter and wrathful. But at the end of his life, you see him refined and grace-filled. That's my heart for you too as you walk through the seven deadly friendships. Yes, you will grieve. Yes, you will have to walk through pain. Yes, you will feel the weight of betrayal. But I would love to see a fourth yes—a yes to the redemptive hand of God in relational heartache.

Looking at Joseph's life and how he walked through his own

pain will empower you to put this book down with hope instead of despair. His behavior and beliefs will show you that it is possible to move on after relationships have utterly broken you—so much so that you become a transformed person who longs to help others find transformation. This is the hard work of discipleship, the rubber meeting the road of living for Jesus in our culture today. Often we see discipleship as religious tasks we do: memorize the Bible, pray consistently, know key verses, be able to share our faith, and give our money for the needs of the church and the world. These tasks can indicate a person's walk with Jesus, but where we really discern a person's character is the way they walk through relational strife. There's a vast difference between being able to quote a Bible verse and choosing to forgive someone who has slain our soul. People hurting us becomes the testing ground of our walk of faith, and Joseph experienced a heap of relational hurt. He, therefore, is a great tutor for us. That's a long way of saying this: Relationships (even difficult ones) are God's means of sanctifying us.

Joseph experienced many things in his long and eventful life, and his traumas involved other people. He grew up loved by his father (preferably so), which got him in trouble with his brothers. For a momentary time, he was a strange marriage of Narcissist Nolan and Dramatic Drake when he shared his vivid dreams in youthful enthusiasm, not realizing he would come across as self-important and a dreamer.

The varied-color coat his father had created for him pushed his brothers toward jealousy and rage. They embodied Predator Paige when the majority of them first wanted to kill him, then settled for selling him into slavery. Judah was the instigator of this transaction. "Judah said to his brothers, 'What profit is it for us to kill our brother and cover up his blood? Come and let us sell him to the Ishmaelites and not lay our hands on him, for he is our brother, our own flesh.' And his brothers listened to him. Then some Midianite traders passed by, so they pulled him up and lifted Joseph out of the pit, and sold him to the Ishmaelites for twenty shekels of silver. Thus they brought Joseph into Egypt" (Genesis 37:26-28 NASB). Selling his brother, Judah resembled Conman Connor.

Joseph encountered Tempter Trevor in the form of his owner Potiphar's wife, who attempted to seduce him. When he ran, she falsely accused him, making her a Faker Fiona. Potiphar, who preferred his wife's story over Joseph's, disregarded the integrity of his servant and sent him to prison, where Joseph gained favor (as he did in Potiphar's house) with the officials there. While there, the very thing that got him into trouble in the first place (dreams) became his eventual salvation when he interpreted the baker and chief cupbearer's dreams. The baker met with demise (as Joseph predicted), and the cupbearer retained his job, promising to tell Pharaoh about Joseph. He didn't share for two years, making him an Unreliable Uma.

Finally, when Pharaoh's dreams could not be discerned and interpreted, the cupbearer remembered Joseph. After Joseph interpreted Pharaoh's dreams to mean seven years of abundance followed by seven years of famine, Pharaoh fulfilled Joseph's earlier dreams of dominance by putting him in charge of most of the kingdom. When Joseph's brothers were on the brink of starvation, they returned to him, not knowing who it was they encountered, and they completed the fulfillment of his teenage dreams by bowing before him.

Everything comes full circle, but not without years of seemingly unremitting pain. In the end, Joseph's trials culminated in the salvation of his people.

Looking back, we see that Joseph was:

- Robed with blessing,
- Robbed through testing,
- Reinstated by entrusting.

This pattern of blessing, testing, and entrusting is instructive for us as we interact with deadly friendships. It helps give us new perspective, making us forward thinking. Joseph remained faithful to God through the trials of broken relationships, even predatory ones.

Let's look at seven words that describe Joseph's life on earth. Ask yourself, *how do these words intersect with my life? My current relationships?*

1. Mocked

2. Abandoned

3. Exploited

4. Betrayed

5. Misunderstood

6. Maligned

7. Imprisoned

Psalm 105:16-22 gives us a snapshot of Joseph's life from God's perspective. It reveals the holy backstory of Joseph's life:

> He called for a famine on the land of Canaan, cutting off its food supply. Then he sent someone to Egypt ahead of them—Joseph, who was sold as a slave. They bruised his feet with fetters and placed his neck in an iron collar. Until the time came to fulfill his dreams, the LORD tested Joseph's character. Then Pharaoh sent for him and set him free; the ruler of the nation opened his prison door. Joseph was put in charge of all the king's household; he became ruler over all the king's possessions. He could instruct the king's aides as he pleased and teach the king's advisers.

In all this we see the beauty and complexity of God's sovereign plan. There was a "so what" to his suffering at the hands of others. Though he encountered many of the seven deadly friendships (and he himself embodied two of them!), God continued to work through him in order to carry out his redemptive plan.

That's the crux of my prayer for you as you walk through a difficult relationship—that you would begin to see God's storytelling in your life even in the midst of pain and bewilderment. My hope is that you can watch the faithfulness of Joseph and let it spur you on toward deep spiritual growth. So much growth can come in discord. The pain we walk through can become a catalyst to push us toward God. I'm reminded of the beauty of Paul's words in 2 Corinthians 11:30: "If I must boast, I would rather boast about the things that show how weak I am." Paul realizes the beautiful paradox that our weakness represents the perfect time to be married to God's strength. Our brokenness is the hello to the healing of Jesus because it means we are beautifully dependent on Jesus. In that dependence, we experience profound growth.

Joseph grew in seven areas of his life. Let these seven terms overshadow the first seven words you read above. Replace *mocked, abandoned, exploited, betrayed, misunderstood, maligned,* and *imprisoned* with these hope-infused descriptions: *filled, forward thinking, fruitful, forgiving, faithful, God-fearing,* and *friendly.*

FILLED

Joseph, despite all his trials and betrayals, turned to God to fill him. He must have learned the lesson Jesus shared that ultimately only God can be fully trusted. "Because of the miraculous signs Jesus did in Jerusalem at the Passover celebration, many began to trust in him. But Jesus didn't trust them, because he knew human nature. No one needed to tell him what mankind is really like" (John 2:23-25). It's interesting to note that Joseph's overflowing life wasn't noticed by God's people, but by Pharaoh. "So Pharaoh asked his officials, 'Can we find anyone else like this man so obviously filled with the spirit of God?'" (Genesis 41:38). The stunning truth for us who intermingle with those who hurt us is that we can still maintain a life that overflows, despite all that's happened. And we can demonstrate faithfulness while the world watches.

Forward Thinking

When Joseph settled in as a leader in Egypt, he married and had two children. What he named them is instructive, since their names serve as storytellers to what Joseph had endured. "Joseph named his older son Manasseh, for he said, 'God has made me forget all my troubles and everyone in my father's family'" (Genesis 41:51). Obviously, from the later narrative, we know Joseph hadn't completely forgotten his family, but in order for him to fulfill the calling God had on his life, he had to let go of them. The past had to be put to rest so he could be forward thinking and move on with power. The same is true for us. Relationships that have marred us have a tendency to shout their influence. But to be able to welcome new people and new experiences, and to fulfill the unique calling God has on our lives during the great right now, we have to let go of the past.

Fruitful

Joseph's second son's name hints at what we may be missing if we don't let go of past relationships that continually haunt us: "Joseph named his second son Ephraim, for he said, 'God has made me fruitful in this land of my grief'" (Genesis 41:52). What a beautiful promise! And how helpful to those of us who pitch a tent in the land of grief! Grief almost always involves a past relationship (whether someone harmed us, or someone we loved has moved or died). In order to move on, we must grieve. Shoving grief down and pretending our sadness doesn't exist (or bootstrapping, convincing ourselves of our own invincibility) will not erase it. Instead, shoving delays its effects. So we grieve, but we don't grieve without hope. God's heart for you is that you would be fruitful even in the center of your grief.

I used to think that I had to have everything in order for God to use me, including all my relationships lined up in a pretty row—no discord, no conflict. But what I've found is that those times of discord and conflict often cause me to grieve, and that grief (when I've been trained by it) pushes me toward the embrace of Jesus. In that embrace, of course, there is fruitfulness, because whenever I'm near Jesus, dependent upon him for everything, I can't help but bear fruit.

FORGIVING

Joseph learned the art of forgiveness during his years of slavery, exile, and imprisonment. Notice the interchange he has with his brothers in Genesis 45:3-4: "'I am Joseph!' he said to his brothers. 'Is my father still alive?' But his brothers were speechless! They were stunned to realize that Joseph was standing there in front of them. 'Please come closer,' he said to them." Instead of running away from them or seeking to banish his brothers forever, Joseph says three important words: *Please come closer.* Those are words of reconciliation and forgiveness.

In one of my most painful relationships with a Narcissist Nolan, I spent several years bound to bitterness. Once, one of my counselors looked directly at me (and into my heart) and told me, "You are very bitter, Mary." And she was right. The Lord used her observation to bring me on a journey. The question she seemed to be asking me was this: Will you be ready to embrace her if she comes back to you? For a long time, I'm sorry to say, I was not ready. I had all sorts of rehearsed speeches involving various versions of "I told you so." But eventually, as God softened my heart, I came to the place where I honestly knew I could ask her to please come closer if she wanted reconciliation. The prayer I'd been praying for her was decades long, and I felt like it would never be answered. But God did some miraculous work in her life behind the scenes, and when she approached me, I was able to step toward her with a forgiving heart.

Faithful

Joseph's fidelity to God is evidenced by the way he speaks to his brothers when they tearfully reunite. He doesn't blame them, but instead points to the orchestration of God's plan. "I am Joseph, your brother, whom you sold into slavery in Egypt. But don't be upset, and don't be angry with yourselves for selling me to this place. It was God who sent me here ahead of you to preserve your lives" (Genesis 45:4-5).

Five chapters later, we hear echoes of the same declaration: "You intended to harm me, but God intended it all for good. He brought me to this position so I could save the lives of many people" (50:20). I tend to be myopic after I encounter a deadly friendship. I can only see how that relationship has harmed me and set me in places I never intended to go. But Joseph remains faithful to God. He has the uncanny ability not to blame others, but to see the handiwork of God's new story. He sees that maybe all this pain isn't about him, but about God's unfolding plan to help others. When his father, Jacob, blesses Joseph in Genesis 49:23-24, we see how deeply he relied on God and his plan: "Archers attacked him savagely; they shot at him and harassed him. But his bow remained taut, and his arms were strengthened by the hands of the Mighty One of Jacob, by the Shepherd, the Rock of Israel."

GOD-FEARING

Connected to Joseph's fidelity is his great fear of God. Note what happens when Potiphar's wife (a Tempter Trevor if there ever was one!) chased after him: "But Joseph refused. 'Look,' he told her, 'my master trusts me with everything in his entire household. No one here has more authority than I do. He has held back nothing from me except you, because you are his wife. How could I do such a wicked thing? It would be a great sin against God'" (Genesis 39:8-9). He didn't say, "I'll get in trouble." Instead he realized that his integrity in this situation was the gift he gave to the Lord. He knew that giving in to her would mean turning his back on God. He feared God far more than he feared her, and the result of his properly placed fear was imprisonment. Wouldn't it be great if our integrity meant a great life? But Tempter Trevors tend to be vindictive, and when they don't convince you to go their way, they are punitive. Even so, God saw Joseph. Though Joseph suffered in the short term for fearing God, he succeeded in the end.

FRIENDLY

Although Joseph took his brothers on a long ride of leaving his presence, returning to their father, and threatening imprisonment for them, when he finally revealed himself to them, his demeanor was kind. He didn't judge them for their sin against him. Instead, he rescued them, their families, and their patriarch (his father), Jacob. When they were terrified once they knew Joseph's true identity, this is how Joseph reacted: "He reassured them by speaking kindly to them" (Genesis 50:21).

You may not experience this sort of reconciliation. There may be people in your life who never return to you. But if they do, and if

God orchestrates a coming together, may Joseph's response of kindness empower you to do the same. We are all broken, sin-scarred, clay-footed people who hurt each other. We are all in need of grace. Once you walk through the long journey of forgiveness, it paves the way for kindness to reign in the way you interact with others. You don't have to be enslaved any longer to vindication and bitterness. Because of how Jesus has intersected your life (and we'll look at him in the next chapter), forgiving your mountain of sin, you will be empowered through the Holy Spirit to forgive the molehill of sin perpetrated against you.

When we look at the life of Joseph, we see an archetype of Jesus. His messy life points us to the Messiah, who also was robed with blessing, robbed through testing, and reinstated by entrusting. Andrew Wilson highlights several of their similarities:

> Joseph, like Jesus, is favored by his father, honored in front of his family, and given a vision of the whole of Israel worshiping him. This prompts jealousy and hatred from his brothers, who conspire to kill him, even as he comes to serve them. Reuben intercedes for him, as Pilate later will for Jesus, but Joseph is eventually thrown into a pit anyway and sold for pieces of silver through the mediation of Judah (whose name, in its Greek form, would be Judas). Blood is presented to Joseph's father— the blood of a goat, the animal which makes atonement in Leviticus.[1]

Like Joseph, Jesus finds safety in the land of Egypt. They both interact with two criminals (the baker, the cupbearer, and the two thieves on the cross). Joseph provides bread to the nation of Israel, while Jesus is the Bread of Life. Both usher in deliverance. Yet Joseph is a man, prone to sin, which is why his life is instructive for us as we suffer, but he cannot come to our aid when we encounter deadly friendships. Only Jesus can do that. Let's look next to him.

9

JESUS

To you who are willing to listen, I say, love your enemies!
Do good to those who hate you. Bless those who curse you.
Pray for those who hurt you. If someone slaps you on one
cheek, offer the other cheek also. If someone demands your
coat, offer your shirt also. Give to anyone who asks; and
when things are taken away from you, don't try to get them
back. Do to others as you would like them to do to you.

LUKE 6:27-31

What I love about Jesus is his empathy. When his words permeate our hearts, we can be assured that he knows what he's talking about. When he tells us to love our enemies, we know that he experienced enemies in his life on earth. We see him constantly turning the other cheek, doing good to those who hated him, blessing those who cursed him behind his back. He not only offered his coat and shirt, but he presented his back to be flogged—the very back that bore the weight of all our sin. Though others treated him with contempt and betrayal, he chose to do unto them through the filter of a surrendered life of love. In short, he experienced relational pain; he demonstrated what love looks like in the midst of it; he empathizes when we experience something similar; and he empowers us to walk with love and forgiveness.

All this empathy is summed up beautifully in Hebrews 4:14-16:

> Since we have a great High Priest who has entered
> heaven, Jesus the Son of God, let us hold firmly to what
> we believe. This High Priest of ours understands our
> weaknesses, for he faced all of the same testings we do,
> yet he did not sin. So let us come boldly to the throne of
> our gracious God. There we will receive his mercy, and
> we will find grace to help us when we need it most.

This same Jesus, though, didn't say we had to be in relation-ship with everyone. We are not to "throw [our] pearls to pigs." (See Matthew 7:6.) He didn't deeply entrust his heart to Pharisees. You see him slipping through the throng of people bent on killing him. Often he withdrew from crowds in order to be with his Father. His is a story of connection with others, yes, but it's also a reminder that relationships don't come with an easy-to-understand blueprint.

When we look at the life of Jesus, we see how he interacted with all of the seven deadly friends.

- The rich young ruler and Narcissist Nolan bear some resemblance. This ruler proudly proclaimed that he didn't sin, then went away dejected because Jesus pointed out the reality of his heart.

- Peter, who swore he would never deny Jesus, became Unreliable Uma as the rooster crowed.

- The disciples often were unreliable, and that trait seemed to augment during the moment Jesus needed them the most as he prayed in the garden of Gethsemane. "He returned to the disciples and found them asleep. He said to Peter, 'Couldn't you watch with me even one hour?'" (Matthew 26:40).

- Obviously, Judas preyed on Jesus, setting circumstances in motion for the beating, mocking, ridicule, and inevitable crucifixion of Jesus. I can think of no better example of Predator Paige.

- Judas also benefited financially from his predatory behavior, giving him the dual distinction of being Conman Connor, having betrayed his friend for money.

- When we see Jesus in the wilderness, he is confronted by a very real Satan who is the author of all Tempter Trevors, the culmination of deceit and enticement.

- The Pharisees epitomized Faker Fiona, Jesus calling them whitewashed tombs—pristine (seemingly) on the outside, but full of decay in their souls.

- Thomas exclaimed this when Jesus and his disciples were about to return to Bethany—a place that had become unsafe: "Let's go, too—and die with Jesus" (John 11:16). You see his penchant for drama in the exchange, making him Dramatic Drake.

Because Jesus is empathetic and has walked dusty roads with deadly friendships, his life not only becomes instructive, but because he now lives within us through the Holy Spirit, it becomes empowering. In John 14:12, we see the stunning announcement that not only will we do the work of Jesus on this earth, but we'll excel beyond it (all because of the Spirit within us): "I tell you the truth, anyone who believes in me will do the same works I have done, and even greater works, because I am going to be with the Father." What a shocking and beautiful promise. All that we learn here about Jesus, we can have through the Holy Spirit. He has not left us alone. We are not helpless.

Like Joseph (and even more so), Jesus suffered. The same seven words that typified the life of Joseph are seen in Technicolor in the life of Jesus. Let's revisit those words again:

1. Mocked

2. Abandoned

3. Exploited

4. Betrayed

5. Misunderstood

6. Maligned

7. Imprisoned

Although we see folks mocking Jesus at the foot of the cross and during his interrogation, Jesus was mocked throughout his lifetime. The people he had grown up with failed to believe in him, and once he left that tiny hometown, people teased him about his humble origins. The Pharisees accused him of driving out demons because he was demon possessed, perhaps the greatest mocking in history, calling the sacred defamed. Jesus was abandoned countless times, but we see it keenly upon his arrest, mock trial, and crucifixion. He suffered alone, all his closest friends terrified and scattered.

Exploited by others, Jesus moved from town to town as folks followed him relentlessly, begging him to heal their sick and demon possessed. So seldom do we ever see anyone concerned for his welfare; instead, the crowd followed him because he could give them health. Judas betrayed him, yes. But consider this: When Jesus took on sin to be a righteous, spotless offering, he took on our sin as well. And we betray him when we sin. In short, Jesus has been betrayed by the entire human race.

In that moment of agony we'll never know or understand, God

the Father had to forsake Jesus, breaking the eternal fellowship of the triune God. The immense loneliness and pain he must have experienced can never be known by us.

How many times was Jesus misunderstood? His entire life most people didn't know who he was or what he was trying to accomplish. Even those who knew him intimately kept thinking about an earthly kingdom, asking to sit on his right and his left, when he was ushering in an entirely new paradigm. He inaugurated that kingdom not by pomp and circumstance, but through humiliation and crucifixion. Hardly a regal way to start a movement. The teachers of religious law, the very ones who should have understood and loved Jesus, instead murmured about him, sowing discord, and endeavoring to kill the very one who would give them life. Not only was Jesus imprisoned before his crucifixion, but he was also imprisoned in the bowels of the earth upon death. In comparison with anyone who has been imprisoned because of someone else's sin against him, Jesus has experienced far worse. Billions of people's sin caused him to pay the penalty, though he was wholly innocent.

I could end this chapter right now, and to be honest, all I want to do is get on my face and worship Jesus. To sing his praises. To thank him day upon day. When the Jewish people celebrate Passover, one of the words they use is *dayenu*. It means, "It would have been enough." Jesus's sufficient sacrifice on the cross is *dayenu*. It is the ultimate of enough. That he also gives those who follow him the Holy Spirit is the buttercream icing on the best cake known to man. Jesus's atonement is enough—even if people betray us, even when someone breaks up with us, even when predators seem to win, even in the midst of genocide and awful war. His sacrifice is enough.

Like Joseph (but to the best extent), Jesus exemplifies being filled, having forward thinking, living fruitfully, embracing forgiveness, exemplifying faithfulness, and acting friendly. He is these things, but he also empowers us to be these things—even after relational heartache.

FILLED

Jesus was obviously filled with the Holy Spirit. After being baptized, we see the embodiment of that in the form of a dove. "Then Jesus, full of the Holy Spirit, returned from the Jordan River. He was led by the Spirit in the wilderness" (Luke 4:1). Note that the Spirit led Jesus into the wilderness where temptation and pain awaited him. Although it's not always understandable why God allows difficult people and situations into our lives, we can know that he will sustain and fill us when we encounter them.

When Jesus meets with the Samaritan woman at the well, we hear more about this metaphor of filling. "If you only knew the gift God has for you and who you are speaking to, you would ask me, and I would give you living water…Anyone who drinks this water will soon become thirsty again. But those who drink the water I give will never be thirsty again. It becomes a fresh, bubbling spring within them, giving them eternal life" (John 4:10,13-14). His filling is not in isolation; it's a promise to all of us that we can be filled—so much so that we can endure temptations, love others, and weather the relational storms of deadly friendships.

FORWARD THINKING

Jesus did everything because he could see the end result—our salvation and God's beautiful glory. He endured hardship, difficult relationships, betrayal, and beatings at the hands of sinful men for the sake of a new life for us. The author of Hebrews reminds us of this powerful truth: "We do this by keeping our eyes on Jesus, the champion who initiates and perfects our faith. Because of the joy awaiting him, he endured the cross, disregarding its shame. Now he is seated in the place of honor beside God's throne" (Hebrews 12:2). He looked forward to the joy awaiting him. This gave him the endurance necessary to walk through hell on earth.

Hebrews reminds us that we have this same wherewithal. We keep our eyes on Jesus, remembering his forward-thinking ways. When we do this, when we seek to see beyond today's pains into tomorrow's sanctification and growth, we are better able to endure hardships at the hands of others. This world is not all there is. The "the end" to your story is not today. The grand story of God has its completion in another world, where there will no longer be weeping and sadness and relational angst.

FRUITFUL

Jesus bore fruit throughout his life, but his greatest fruit is you and me. We are the fruit of his sacrifice, the culmination of his raucous act on the cross. He spent his life deeply connected to his Father, watching what the Father was doing so he could walk in the same manner. We have that similar mandate, to know God and bear fruit. Jesus said this in John 15:4-5: "Remain in me, and I will remain in you. For a branch cannot produce fruit if it is severed from the vine, and you cannot be fruitful unless you remain in me. Yes, I am the vine; you are the branches. Those who remain in me, and I in them, will produce much fruit. For apart from me you can do nothing."

Fruitfulness is dependent on connectedness. And because of what Jesus did on the cross, we have unfettered access to him. We can right now be connected to the Vine. And all who are connected to the Vine bear fruit. Look at how Paul defines fruit in Galatians 5:22-25:

> The Holy Spirit produces this kind of fruit in our lives: love, joy, peace, patience, kindness, goodness, faithfulness, gentleness, and self-control. There is no law against these things! Those who belong to Christ Jesus have nailed the passions and desires of their sinful nature to his cross and crucified them there. Since we are living by the Spirit, let us follow the Spirit's leading in every part of our lives.

Note that this kind of fruit is relational in nature. It's hard to love without people in your life to demonstrate that love to. How can you exhibit gentleness without someone to be gentle with? How do we become fruitful in this way? We follow the Spirit of God who causes the fruit.

FORGIVING

We all know Jesus is forgiving. His trek to the cross demonstrates that. He chose to offer himself so we could be forgiven of our myriad sins. But even from the cross when his agony was at its peak, Jesus said, "Father, forgive them, for they don't know what they are doing" (Luke 23:34). Because of this kind of radical forgiveness, we can now forgive others. What we've received, we freely give. (See the parable of the two debtors in Luke 7:36-50 for a poignant cautionary tale of this.) Forgiveness, though, is not simply a "one and done" act. It's layered and often complicated. We think we've forgiven, only to be hurt again by a deadly friendship, and we have more forgiving to do. It doesn't mean you chase someone back into relationship, particularly if they're predatory. Forgiveness should not be forced (meaning someone else cannot simply demand that you forgive their behavior). But as you grapple with forgiving those friends who have deeply hurt you, you'll be set free from bitterness and an unhealthy tie to them. In short, bitterness keeps you connected to the one who hurt you. Forgiveness is the scissors that cut that tie.

FAITHFUL

Jesus was faithful to his Father and his mission. He accomplished what God called him to do. He obeyed to the point of death.

In order to be faithful, he stayed close to the Father. "I tell you the truth, the Son can do nothing by himself. He does only what he sees the Father doing. Whatever the Father does, the Son also does" (John 5:19). Later, in John 6:38, he affirms, "I have come down from heaven to do the will of God who sent me, not to do my own will." Perhaps that's one of the most difficult parts of dealing with deadly friendships—they steer us away from doing what God has called us to do. Many times, the disciples (wrongly) sought to deter Jesus from his mission. In one particular incident right after Peter says that Jesus is the Christ, he begins to tell Jesus to stop talking about what would await him in Jerusalem. Jesus's rebuke was swift: "Get away from me, Satan! You are a dangerous trap to me. You are seeing things merely from a human point of view, not from God's" (Matthew 16:23).

Perhaps some of your deadlier friendships are acting in a similar way, deterring you from the work God has called you to do. They've become a sideshow distraction, one that woos you away from God's work. Jesus's example of going to the Father first is helpful here. He should be our first relationship, our first allegiance. Faithfulness to him matters.

GOD-FEARING

Jesus feared God more than he feared others. Of utmost importance was God's opinion of him. Had he followed the popular advice of his time, particularly from the Pharisees, he would have established an earthly kingdom, but not an eternal one. In Luke 22:42 when he is agonizing about the cross before him, he prays, "Father, if you are willing, please take this cup of suffering away from me. Yet I want your will to be done, not mine." He knew the suffering would be awful, but he wanted God's will more than anything else.

And that's entirely helpful as we endure difficult and toxic relationships with grace. Above all, we learn to fear God's opinion more than others. If we spend our lives worrying about the opinions of others, we'll spend our lives in reputation management—a tiring and trying pursuit. But if we seek the heart of God in everything we do, having a firm fidelity to him first, we'll gain the right perspective about our difficult relationships. If our goal is God's glory above all, we will be trained to find joy in the midst of relational trials.

FRIENDLY

Jesus was joyful. Still is. But we forget this because of how we've seen him portrayed. Somber and sullen. Morose and introspective. But consider this: Children loved to spend time with Jesus. He was friendly, kind, welcoming, and irresistible. Why else would everyone seek to follow him when he walked the dusty roads of Bethany? He chose to woo us to himself because of his kindness. Titus 3:4-5 confirms this beautiful truth: "When God our Savior revealed his kindness and love, he saved us, not because of the righteous things we had done, but because of his mercy. He washed away our sins, giving us a new birth and new life through the Holy Spirit."

And that's the perfect way to end this look at Jesus's life. He is kind. He empowers us to be kind. We don't have to let the relational distress of the past inform the way we interact with people today. We cannot do this on our own. In our paltry strength, we are unkind, vindictive, and sometimes broken, seemingly beyond repair. But because of the "new birth and new life through the Holy Spirit," we can love our enemies and pray for those who persecute us. Jesus demonstrated that kindness, and the Holy Spirit gives us the power to live a kind life.

We can demonstrate all these traits even after relational pain because he is all these things, and he will give us these abilities. We can move on. We can let go of the pain. But here's the upside-down truth about the pain you've endured at the hands of deadly friendships: That pain has a promise to it. When someone's sin has placed us in a pit, we can reach up for God's help. The pain pit is the means for us to reach up. Our weakness isn't something God despises. Instead, it's the very avenue to experience his marvelous power and healing. I love what Paul writes in 1 Corinthians 1:26-31 (NIV). I'm pretty sure I've quoted these verses in every book I've written because they're so powerful.

> Brothers and sisters, think of what you were when you were called. Not many of you were wise by human standards; not many were influential; not many were of noble birth. But God chose the foolish things of the world to shame the wise; God chose the weak things of the world to shame the strong. God chose the lowly things of this world and the despised things—and the things that are not—to nullify the things that are, so that no one may boast before him. It is because of him that you are in Christ Jesus, who has become for us wisdom from God—that is, our righteousness, holiness and redemption. Therefore, as it is written: "Let the one who boasts boast in the Lord."

Your relational pain is the means for Jesus to do his best work in and through you. It's not a detriment or a demerit; it's the means by which Jesus empowers you.

Because he understands. He's been there. He's walked through every deadly friendship to the deepest and most painful degree. He knows how to come alongside those who hurt. And through his Holy Spirit, he gives you the grace and grit to weather whatever difficult relationship entangles you. That doesn't mean you won't hurt or agonize or make bad decisions. But it does mean you have a companion to walk with you, even in the trenches of difficult relationships. Oh, how Jesus knows!

10

The Seven Life-Giving Practices

You prepare a feast for me in the presence of my enemies.

Psalm 23:5

Writing a book about deadly friendships felt daunting. After all, wouldn't I be delving into the darkness? Would all that research sap me of life? Although at times I experienced the weight of the plunge, what has happened instead is wholly surprising. Jesus reminds us of this important truth: Life springs from decay. "I tell you the truth, unless a kernel of wheat is planted in the soil and dies, it remains alone. But its death will produce many new kernels—a plentiful harvest of new lives" (John 12:24). Life and vitality come from the ashes of death, and therein is our hope. You may have been wounded in difficult community, but when you connect to perfect community (Jesus) and healthy imperfect community (safe people), you have the profound potential to revive.

We've looked at the seven deadly friendships (Narcissist Nolan, Unreliable Uma, Predator Paige, Conman Connor, Tempter Trevor, Faker Fiona, and Dramatic Drake) based on Proverbs 6:16-19: "There are six things the LORD hates—no, seven things he detests: haughty eyes, a lying tongue, hands that kill the innocent, a heart that plots evil, feet that race to do wrong, a false witness who pours

175

out lies, a person who sows discord in a family." We've learned to discern who they are, how they entrap us, and how we can extricate ourselves from those relationships or learn to deal with them in a forward-thinking manner. We've heard stories of broken people on both sides of friendship. And to be sure, we have all bent toward dysfunction because 100 percent of humanity is broken and flawed. We are not the hero and everyone else the perpetrator. We are both, and we need hope.

I believe God wants to bring you life, to revive your fervor, to give you a new perspective, even though you've faced betrayal, pain, and harsh words from others—things that have felt like death. A broken friendship need not ruin everything about today, and it can prove to be a catalyst for new growth. Instead of viewing your painful relationship through the lens of lack, begin to see it as an avenue toward a life of wholeness, wisdom, and purpose.

But how?

As I've walked through my own deadly friendships (sometimes very poorly), I've learned a lot in the aftermath. This book began with death metaphors, but it ends with life-giving ones. Which is why there are seven positive things you can do, seven life-giving practices that will not only help you navigate a difficult friendship, but will also change the way you view your life. These have been gleaned from Scripture, hard-won wisdom, and observation over the years. The principles spell *revival*, a beautiful word indeed.

- Review your past.
- Embrace new healing.
- Verify your expectations.
- Invert their behavior.
- Vocalize your journey.

- Assess current relationships.
- Live life forward.

REVIEW YOUR PAST

In order to grow through a negative relationship (or a series of harmful friendships), it's imperative you find out why you keep chasing after these types of toxic relationships. This has been key in my own healing. As I've mentioned before, I'm constantly trying to complete incomplete stories by pursuing the types of people who rejected me in childhood. I naively think that if I can attract, change, and win one of those types of deadly friendships, I can somehow prove myself worthy of love.

The problem with that approach is that it works zero percent of the time. Chasing narcissists will never reform them, they can never love you, and you'll end up with more open-ended, unfinished stories—all while your heart shreds to pieces. This is why it's important to get at the root of your pursuit. Heal that, and you heal your pursuit.

Time travel to those places in your past when people deeply wounded you. Ask yourself if they have some traits similar to your current deadly friendships. If they correspond, begin to ask Jesus to complete your broken story with himself. Only he can give you worth, show you your value, and endow you with significance. He fashioned you, knows you, and loves you. He is for you. Letting him complete your story gives you the health needed to make better decisions later.

In other words, if I know I am worthy and loved right now in this moment because of what Jesus has done in my life, I am better able to say no when someone wants to harm me. I'll create proper fences around myself with a strong gate that lets in the good people, but shuts it to people who want to harm me. If I have settled my worth in the embrace of Jesus, I will want to treat myself kindly, which translates into the relationships I pursue.

Shahida Arabi, an expert in narcissistic relationships, reminds us how normal this all is—why we gravitate toward that which was familiar:

> If we were scapegoated as children, we'll feel a sense of toxic shame and pervasive unworthiness that prevents us from knowing we deserve better…When we get tangled up with a narcissist who could possibly be the mirror image of one or both of our parents, we revert back to that sense of powerlessness and shame that plagued us ever since we were young children…While the logical, reasoning part of our brain tells us to get out, our subconscious runs towards the very perpetrator who acts and behaves an awful lot like the ones that we depended on for our survival.[1]

What is familiar is what entices us, which is why we must unpack our why—why do we gravitate toward those who hurt us? Who do they remind us of? What story are we trying to complete? And how can Jesus fill the broken, needy parts of us so we don't keep pursuing the same deadly friendships?

Some have thrown around the word *codependent* in cases like these, where we keep running back to the same people, enabling them and empowering them to act unbecomingly. But perhaps that label is unhelpful. Arabi contends, "Codependency is a term historically used to describe interactions between addicts and their loved ones, not victims and their abusers. Dr. Clare Murphy (2016) asserts that abuse victims can actually exhibit codependent traits *as a result of trauma*, not because they are, in fact, codependent."[2] Perhaps it's time to offer yourself some grace instead of believing a label others have carelessly attached to you. People who hurt other people are highly skilled at exploitation. They're good at it, and they get away with abusive behavior. Just because you succumbed to their predatory ways doesn't make you codependent.

Arabi continues, "Contrary to popular myth, *anyone* can be victimized by an abuser—even someone with strong boundaries initially, because covert abuse is insidious and unbelievably traumatic."[3]

It's time to be kind to yourself. In looking back, consider how you've treated yourself. Perhaps the person you need to make peace with is *you*. Maybe you believe you deserve ill treatment, and you've spent a lifetime yelling at yourself internally, berating yourself into sadness. Maybe you've been a deadly friend to yourself! You feel you deserve such treatment. So when someone reemphasizes your lack of worth, it feels hauntingly familiar—like your own internal voice. This has become a sad pattern, one that Paul recognized in the Corinthian believers: "After all, you think you are so wise, but you enjoy putting up with fools! You put up with it when someone enslaves you, takes everything you have, takes advantage of you, takes control of everything, and slaps you in the face" (2 Corinthians 11:19-20).

Dick Foth reminds us of the importance of loving ourselves well by seeking that love first from God: "If we are not experiencing God's love, we will always be seeking from others what only God can give. They will always fail us because we have expectations from the friendships that they cannot meet."[4]

Henry Nouwen agrees:

> I discovered the real problem—expecting from a friend what only Christ can give…Friendship requires closeness, affection, support, and mutual encouragement, but also distance, space to grow, freedom to be different, and solitude. To nurture both aspects of a relationship,

> we must experience a deeper and more lasting affirma-
> tion than any human relationship can offer...When we
> truly love God and share in his glory, our relationships
> lose their compulsive character.[5]

To grow while we face deadly friendships, we must first look at our patterns of running to people in the past (instead of running to God). This sprint typically happens when we're afraid. One helpful exercise: Look back on the times in your life when you were terri-fied. Who did you pursue? What types of people did you gravitate to? Why? And how were you unkind to yourself during that time of fear? Journaling may help you see your deeply ingrained patterns of behavior. Asking other healthy friends or a counselor will also help you discern your past behaviors. Once you understand these, you can begin to set things right.

When someone has a disease, they can either pay for over-the-counter medicines and mask the symptoms or deal with the root cause. Many of us put bandages on our patterns of behavior, think-ing that perhaps that will help. We take cough drops, but the cough continues. What we need is healing from the inside out, to address the actual underlying disease. Looking at your past may not initially solve your penchant for seeking love in all the wrong places, but it is the first step (and the most important step) on the healing journey.

EMBRACE NEW HEALING

We all need relational healing. Unfortunately, we think isola-tion brings healing. We reason, if people hurt us, then avoiding people will mean less hurt. Not true. When I speak to audiences about broken relationships, I often say, "What wounds you is what heals you." We are wounded in community, yet we are also healed in community. The key is identifying unsafe and safe communities, something we'll tackle in Assess Current Relationships (see page 188). But before we identify who is safe and who is not, we must recognize when we've walled off our hearts from everyone. There's a difference between a fence (that keeps intruders out and safe people in) and a fortress—a heart that keeps everyone at bay.

Healing is something Jesus wants for you. Watch how he interacted with crowds when he walked the earth. He was constantly healing people, setting them free, giving them hope. He loves to heal us. But so often, we've grown sadly accustomed to discord and dysfunction. It's become our happy, knowable place so much so that growth and healing terrify us because they are unknown. We know how to deal with people who harm us; we don't know how to live with people who are blessings to us.

There is no such thing as passive healing. You can't lackadaisically heal. You have to want to get well, coming to a place in your life where your sadness over your past relationships trumps your need for life stranded in the status quo. You may have experienced post-traumatic stress in your relationships, and you trigger easily. If that's the case, searching out a trusted and licensed counselor will be a huge boon to your healing journey. I firmly believe that PTSD doesn't have to lead to continued bad choices in relationships. Instead, let's embrace PTG: post-traumatic growth.

One of the things that prevents healing in our relationships is what Martin Seligman calls learned helplessness—"instances in which an organism has learned that outcomes are uncontrollable by his response and is seriously debilitated by this knowledge."[6] When we encounter pain due to difficult, toxic relationships, we can begin to feel that we'll never have a different life. We are helpless and hapless. We believe (wrongly) that things will always be this way, that we'll always choose people who harm us. This leads to a deficit mind-set: *I deserve these kinds of friends.*

When we give in to this thinking, we begin to believe that not even God can pull us out or rescue us. But the truth is, healing is available. New life can spring from the dregs of past bad choices. Sometimes we can be so overwhelmed by the trauma of the past that we cannot see any other choice.

I once had a frustrating dream. When I woke from it, I realized how I'd been giving in to learned helplessness about a relationship I had with a narcissistic person. In the dream, I was desperately trying to push a minivan to the airport about 18 miles away. No one in the vehicle would help me, and the task loomed impossible. Still, I kept trying. I wrongly believed that if I had no success now, somehow I could finagle that elusive success if I just kept trying harder.

When I woke up, the solution seemed obvious to me. I should have called a cab. No one can push a minivan 18 miles successfully, at least not in the time needed to grab our airplane. We can be so intent on staying in our old patterns that we can't see the obvious way through. Which also helps me realize that I need the Lord in the healing journey, and I need positive, life-affirming relationships.

Verify Your Expectations

Our level of happiness in life depends upon our management of expectations, particularly in relationships. If we expect Narcissist Nolan to be kind and attentive to us, we'll be constantly sad and disappointed. But if we understand that he can never really think of anyone but himself, we'll have a healthier view of his capabilities. We won't demand that he meet an impossible standard.

Unrealistic expectations don't merely affect our relationships with deadly friends. They infuse our current healthy relationships too. My husband and I were counseling a younger couple, and this issue came up. Both coming from difficult backgrounds, they'd created an idealized picture of what they wanted marriage to be—more specifically, how they wanted each other to behave. Their impossibly high personal expectations projected outward toward each other. We talked about managing expectations. Our pastor, Steve Stroope, has often shared about the expectation gap. Our happiness is directly measured by the gap between our expectations and reality. The wider the gap, the less happy we are. So in choosing to lower your friendship expectations, you'll place less pressure on your friends to make you happy.

But you also don't want to swing wildly to zero expectations. When you give up all expectations, you open yourself up for abusive relationships. If you accept every bit of negative behavior, internalizing someone else's predation, you'll begin to believe you deserve negative treatment. Expectations aren't bad; they need to be in place. They just need not be impossible.

Rosie has some wise advice for those of us burdened by high expectations:

> I hear this sentiment echoed often on Facebook and in memes, but I don't seem to experience much disappointment in this area. I think it's because I don't expect my friends to be responsible for supporting me. If they do, I am so grateful and impressed by their care and concern. If they don't, I don't think I notice too much, because God always supplies someone—and usually not the someone I expected—to be there.

A wise woman pulled her aside when Rosie was struggling with her mother.

> She said that if my *deserve level* was high and people responded below what I expected, then I'd always be disappointed. But if my *deserve level* was set lower (or at zero),

then everything people did for me became icing. That advice revolutionized my thinking. All friends are not created equal. They aren't always available when I need them. Some are very intuitive and others centered. They are most likely to see and serve. Others are wrapped up in their own troubles. I also give a lot of grace because I'm not always the most proactive friend when someone is going through a trial—and then other times I am. I believe, though, that some friends are made for the fun times and some are first-responder types when there is a need. I can't expect them to think like me or react like I would.

Karen also experienced this rejuvenation of realistic expectations:

A wise-beyond-her-youth friend told me when we were in our early twenties that there are many kinds of friends. There are shopping friends. There are friends who will clean your bathroom when you had surgery. There are friends who will meet you for coffee once a month, just to catch up. There are friends who will truly pray for you, faithfully. There are "kindergarten" friends who you can skip seeing for thirty-five years and then pick up where you left off and laugh and laugh and laugh.

In light of that, Karen has adjusted her expectations.

I simply don't expect my "she'll visit me in the hospital" friend to be my "garage sale jaunting" friend. Plus, even tried-and-true friends have needs and circumstances that change over time, as each of us does. So what happens when your garage sale jaunting friend runs out of steam? Maybe she's gone from your life, if that's all you had in common. Or maybe she knows you so well and loves you so much that she's become your best prayer partner, and you don't even realize it.

The fluidity of friendships and the inevitability of change help us adjust our expectations. But what happens when a deadly friendship threatens to steal more than we can give? What do we do when even our minimized expectations are continually shunned, and our deadly friendship keeps injuring us over and over again? As I've mentioned in the narcissist and predatory chapters, in these cases it's often best to let go of the friendship—for your sake. I never understood the passages where the disciples shook the dust off their feet, or the fact that Jesus instructed them to do so, until I experienced yet another difficult friendship. Sometimes you just need to shake the pain away in order to move on to a new place and find healing. Jesus instructed in Matthew 10:14 (NASB) that "whoever does not receive you, nor heed your words, as you go out of that house or that city, shake the dust off your feet." It's a symbolic letting go, but for us in pain-infusing friendships, shaking the dust means a breakup.

I love the juxtaposition of Acts 13:51 (NASB) with verse 52, from dust to joy: "But they shook off the dust of their feet in protest against them and went to Iconium. And the disciples were continually filled with joy and with the Holy Spirit." Could it be that we should live this contrast? To shake toxic friendships, yet choose to joyfully venture forth in the aftermath? That's my prayer for you— that you'll manage your expectations, yes, but that you'll also gain wisdom and discernment about shaking the dust. And when you let go of destructive relationships, joy will follow.

INVERT THEIR BEHAVIOR

One of the most painful things I've encountered in my own life was discovering my own narcissism. The very thing I swore I would not be, I became to a certain degree. My tendency has been to introspect to the point of obsessing about myself, which then turns everything inward. Thankfully, I have wise friends and a good husband who help me see when I'm circling only around myself. They kindly remind me when I'm nudging close to narcissistic behavior. I see this same tendency in others, particularly those who were raised by toxic parents. The very thing they hated in their parents becomes their behavior as adults. But just like learned helplessness can make us feel like this is inevitable, Jesus's intersection in our lives produces a counterintuitive reversal: We don't have to become our deadly friend.

We can, by the Holy Spirit, move in the opposite manner of the one insulting us. Jesus spoke about this in the Sermon on the Mount where he talks about returning evil with good, turning our cheek, and blessing those who curse us. Proverbs is chock full of this kind of inversion, responding in a disarming (calming) way. "A fool is quick-tempered, but a wise person stays calm when insulted" (Proverbs 12:16). "Avoiding a fight is a mark of honor; only fools insist on quarreling" (Proverbs 20:3). "Hatred stirs up quarrels, but love makes up for all offenses" (Proverbs 10:12). "Starting a quarrel is like opening a floodgate, so stop before a dispute breaks out" (Proverbs 17:14). We are not doomed to retaliate in kind. We are empowered to react with winsome hope. Besides Proverbs' prescription to disarm fools and Jesus's admonition to live this kind of inverted reaction, Peter reminds us, "Don't repay evil for evil. Don't retaliate with insults when people insult you. Instead, pay them back with a blessing" (1 Peter 3:9). That is what God has called us all to do—to forsake retaliation and embrace blessing.

When we react negatively to a person who is toxic, it hints at our need for control. And in that place of control, all sorts of bad behaviors flourish. When we seek to exert control, we fall into the very words and actions we despise in the other. When things are going sour in a relationship, my tendency is to want to control an outcome. Instead of praying or choosing to gently talk through an issue, I make assumptions about the other person (often wrong), internally judge them, then try to exert control to "change" them. As you may know, this never works. Why do we keep trying to control when we know it really messes things up? That's when the power of inversion comes into play. We do what the other doesn't expect in an act of surrender of control.

For instance, if Predator Paige tells us again how stupid we are, how unworthy and petty our hearts are, we have a choice. We can try to control what she says by silencing her, or speaking over her, telling her how awful she is, or we can leave the room. But instead of panicking and giving in to fear, which leads to a desire to control, we step back from the situation and weigh it. We might throw a prayer heavenward and ask God for a new way of responding. We might choose, instead, to praise something in another person. We might thank her for her honesty. The truth is, you cannot control Predator Paige's tongue or behavior, but you can control how you respond. You may not be able to control the onslaught of words coming from someone's mouth, but you can control listening. You can control how her hurtful words affect you.

When you embrace the inverting principle, you have more choices—even how you think about your interaction a few days later. Your predatory friend may have spoken lies over you, laced with hatred, but you do not need to live in the light of those lies. You can acknowledge they are lies, tell yourself the truth (you are fearfully and wonderfully made; God loves you; he is making you new) and move on. Don't let a predator win twice—in the moment of the outburst, and for the rest of your life when you wrongly believe their lies.

One thing I've learned over the years is the power of the stake in the ground. Growing up in a home where I felt neglected and unwanted,

I decided that when I had a family, my children would know they were loved. I drove a stake in the ground as an act of remembrance. Instead of letting someone's bad behavior become the blueprint for my later choices, it became the catalyst for holy gumption. Not on my watch. Not in my life. We don't need to sit back and allow someone else's torment to become the way we interact with others. Let their negative example become your stake in the ground, your declaration (with God's help) that you will not be that way. In this way, you can ironically see your difficult friendship as a gift. It has helped you to clarify what you don't want to become. And you absolutely have the choice to drive that stake in the ground and be someone different.

VOCALIZE YOUR JOURNEY

When I speak to audiences, I share this simple truth: An untold story never heals. Your woundedness in relationship is healed through positive relationship, and that involves sharing your heart with someone else. In that space, you begin to see why you felt crazy in the difficult friendship.

This happened to me recently. I had all sorts of conflicting emotions about a predatory friend, but I could not put my finger on why I felt that way. Something wasn't right—and whenever I spent time with her, I was left feeling depleted and confused. So I shared my story with two safe friends. As the words left my mouth, I realized (finally!) that I'd been in a relationship with a predator. Keeping everything inside me did me no good. It only bred confusion, but letting out what I was walking through brought blessed clarity.

Maybe you don't have a safe person in your life with whom you can process your vocalization. That's also okay. Consider writing everything out. Make lists if that is easier. Start by sharing how you feel around the person when you're with him and then out of his presence. Define why you feel ambivalent or confused. Recount some of your conversations. List the facts of your most recent interaction. Seeing it all in black and white can also be a strong catalyst to make some changes.

It's not merely enough to vocalize or journal your friendship breakup or heartache. You may also need to work through your bitterness and anger. Begin by sharing that grief with Jesus as Job did when his friends were hurting him. "I cannot keep from speaking. I must express my anguish. My bitter soul must complain" (Job 7:11). "My friends scorn me, but I pour out my tears to God" (16:20).

God already knows your deepest feelings and fears. Telling him doesn't let the cat out of the bag (you won't take him by surprise), and in that circle of two, you'll begin the process of working through your bitterness. You may also need the reasoned voice and wisdom of a friend to help you process your grief. Bitterness and anger are simply outcomes of being harmed, and grief is the end result and must be worked through. The question that helps me when I'm facing my own hard-hearted bitterness is this: What could I do with the space left behind by letting go of my anger and bitterness?

Vocalizing also means apologizing when you've wronged your deadly friendship. This isn't easy, nor should you approach doing so without prayer from others and wisdom from wise counsel. Predatory friends tend to take your humility and turn it on you. (In this case, if you feel convicted that you need to apologize, it might be better to write it out in a letter instead of face-to-face.) However you choose, the confession will be good for your soul. Paul reminds us, "Do all that you can to live in peace with everyone" (Romans 12:18), and apologizing assures you of that.

Another caveat about apology: You might be like me and have an overactive conscience. You may be one of those people who over-apologizes for everything just to keep the peace. This is not the same as a healthy apology. Sometimes overapologizers need to consult with a wise friend to see if they need to apologize because their script in their head is overcritical.

Overapologizing lets people who hurt others get away with it and justify their behavior. *See? He apologized! My anger was justified. Now I don't have to look at my own issues!* So just be careful as you approach apology. Remember, conviction from God (not from others' accusations per se) is what matters, and God's conviction always comes with *hope*. It's about your specific words or actions, but is never pervasive.

God's specific conviction: Losing your temper in this argument did not represent the fruit of the Spirit. An apology is in order to restore the relationship.

Pervasive script: You're an angry loser who doesn't deserve good relationships. Best grovel back in hope someone, anyone, will befriend you.

See the difference in the tone?

Although we don't always vocalize our forgiveness (some people we forgive are dead), it's important that we walk the journey of forgiveness. I say *journey* because forgiveness isn't always immediate, and it usually doesn't happen in the moment (exception: when parents force two of their children to make up with each other and forgive). But it is the necessary oxygen to relationships, and it is a vital practice as you forge new friendships. Sometimes people demand forgiveness, but that is not something you should ever feel forced to offer. Your choice to forgive is best wrestled through in quiet, after you've had some time to process the hurt, give it to Jesus, and have gained some perspective. Once you've walked through the needed space and introspection to forgive, pray about an opportunity to grant that forgiveness in person. Reconciliation thrives in the soil of stated forgiveness. This is your part of the reconciliation process. You cannot force someone to forgive you, but you can grant forgiveness to the person who has harmed you, face-to-face.

And even if you've forgiven, remember that another outburst may make you think you haven't forgiven because a new offense has poisoned past forgiveness. In that moment, try to tell yourself this: *No, I actually have made the choice to forgive. This new conflict just means another layer of forgiveness I need to walk through. It does not negate my past choice to forgive.*

Let's say my friend Joyce told me she thought I was insensitive and stingy because I didn't readily lend my car to her. Then she calls me names. Now let's say Joyce had a bad day prior to her request and outburst and later requests forgiveness for saying those words to me. If the offense is trivial and seldom happens, I could easily grant that forgiveness right away. But if the interaction is one of a series of bully words Joyce has continued to voice, I could instead say, "Joyce, thanks for bringing this up. I love being a forgiving person, but I've found it's best for me to spend a little time away processing what you've said. Sometimes I need a bit of time to grieve, ask Jesus for help, and move forward. I absolutely value our relationship. Can we circle back to this conversation next week?"

Remember, forgiveness on your part doesn't always equal reconciliation. You can choose to forgive on your side, but that doesn't mean the other person will move toward you in forgiveness. (Sometimes I pray this: *Jesus, please help [the other person] to forgive me—not for my sake necessarily, but for theirs.*) It doesn't guarantee you'll be friends again. But to keep your conscience clear, work through your pain and ask Jesus to help you forgive the other. You do *not* want to live a life of angry bitterness.

For those of you who have been victims of Predator Paige, forgiveness does *not* mean you must reenter relationship. Most of the time, forgiveness is an act you choose for your own soul (with the help of Jesus). If someone perpetrates against you, then demands both forgiveness and immediate relationship or trust, your best response for the sake of your health is to walk away. This is a big world, full of amazing people. You do not need to spend your life interacting with predators or perpetrators.

The last way to vocalize your journey is prayer. Pray for your deadly friendships. Ask God to give you insight into their injury. You may become estranged from your friend, but nothing can stop you from praying for him or her. And letting out your own angst helps you place your pain in the hands of God.

Like the psalmist, I recognized that my honesty brought relief. "Consider, Lord, how your servants are disgraced! I carry in my heart the insults of so many people" (Psalm 89:50). I also love how prayer ushered in restoration for Job. His friends gave him awful advice when he was walking through the most painful time in his life, even blaming him for his trials. They were not good friends, fluctuating between Unreliable Uma and Dramatic Drake. In fact, God rebuked Job's friends. "After the LORD had finished speaking to Job, he said to Eliphaz the Temanite: 'I am angry with you and your two friends, for you have not spoken accurately about me, as my servant Job has'" (Job 42:7). But look at this turn of events: "When Job prayed for his friends, the LORD restored his fortunes" (Job 42:10). There is power in praying for those who wronged you. Praying rightly puts the burden onto God's capable shoulders. Your heart and mind aren't meant to carry all that heartache around. I worry that you may be carrying a relational burden God never intended you to bear. Let go. Place your broken relationship in the hands of Jesus. This is something you *can* control.

ASSESS CURRENT RELATIONSHIPS

As I've written before, what wounds you (negative community) is what heals you (safe community). It's imperative that we learn how to assess what's going on in our current relationships, to see whether the people we surround ourselves with are safe and good for our souls. Remember this simple analogy: A bird alone tires easily, but a flock empowers that same bird to soar.

I want you to soar with safe people. I want you to begin to choose the kinds of friendships that bring you vitality. Proverbs 12:26 reminds us of the importance of making good friendship choices: "The righteous choose their friends carefully, but the way of the wicked leads them astray" (NIV). Henri Nouwen, a Catholic writer, gives us a stunning hint of what that kind of safe community looks like. "We have probably wondered in our many lonesome moments if there is one corner in this competitive, demanding world where it is safe to be relaxed, to expose ourselves to someone else, and to give unconditionally. It might be very small and hidden. But if this corner exists, it calls for a search through the complexities of our human relationships in order to find it."[7]

But how do we choose our friends carefully? And how do we assess our current relationships? We need to know the traits of safe people. I wrote about these types of relationships in *Not Marked: Finding Hope and Healing after Sexual Abuse.*

Safe people...

- Ask clarifying questions.
- Don't jump to conclusions. They assume positive intent. Job 6:29 says, "Stop assuming my guilt, for I have done no wrong."
- Aren't passive-aggressive.
- Empathize with you, not needing to interject their own story of doom to one-up you.
- Encourage other relationships.
- Honor and encourage your relationship with God.

- Want what is best for you and your healing journey (don't have their own healing agenda, or pressure you to heal their way).
- Aren't domineering.
- Tell the truth, even if it's painful, but they tell it in a winsome way.
- Offer grace.
- Are self-aware.
- Reveal their flaws.
- Aren't defensive.
- Apologize, even before they're caught.
- Take responsibility for themselves.
- Work on their own issues.
- Want to learn from their mistakes.
- Accept blame.
- Avoid gossip.
- Are humble, teachable.
- Have a positive influence over your life.
- Have proven themselves trustworthy over a period of time.
- Are the same person in different situations—consistent.
- Applaud your growth.
- Don't try to be your parent or the Holy Spirit.
- Love freedom.
- Don't demand trust—instead they earn it by consistently acting honorable.[8]

May these traits empower you to not only choose good friendships (yes, you do have a choice), but may they also encourage you to become a safe person to your friends. What a different world we would all live in if everyone adopted the traits of a safe person!

You may say, "But my deadly friendships are actually members of my family. What do I do then?" Of course, seeking the wisdom of others is helpful here, but also realize that you may need to separate in order to heal. An unsafe person is an unsafe person whether they're related to you or not. The prophet Jeremiah warned about this very thing. "Even your brothers, members of your own family, have turned against you. They plot and raise complaints against you. Do not trust them, no matter how pleasantly they speak" (Jeremiah 12:6). Trusting an unsafe person will only usher in more hurt, which then results in trauma, bitterness, and a longer road of healing. Be cautious of holding your family to different standards than your friends. A predatory person will prey upon you, no matter the bloodlines.

Shannon Thomas refers to two ways to deal with deadly friendships—no contact and detached contact. No contact means simply that: no connection or contact ever again, whatsoever. Detached contact is not as cut and dried and is often more nuanced and difficult—often used when you still need to see your spouse for child visitations, or you work with the person, or the deadly friendship is part of your family of origin. She equates no contact to an alcoholic who never again touches alcohol, and detached contact as someone who manages an eating disorder (you cannot *not* have food). She writes, "Through no contact, survivors can find ever-increasing distance from the malice that almost permanently ruined their lives. The other journey, detached contact, is the consistent process of living lives of healing while still facing antagonists, but with limited emotional engagement."[9] Deciding which route to take involves wise counsel, prayer, and recognizing where you are emotionally. I have experienced both forms. I have detached when the relationship was caustic to my soul, and I have learned to coexist in detached contact when the person lived in the same town as me. Either way, I've learned the importance of healing from my interaction—whether by walking fully away or preparing myself ahead of time in case I ran into my deadly friendship.

Live Life Forward

Living forward means taking that backward glance, but not staying there. We began the revival process by seeing what shaped us to engage in toxic friendships, but we need not remain in that place. Doing so keeps us tethered to the past, often doomed to repeat the same bad friendship decisions. Instead, we must look forward. We don't need to allow someone else's dysfunction to dictate our current choices. We have the right and the will to choose to rise above for the sake of our future life.

I know it's hard. I've spent many years letting other people's issues taint my days. In other words, their actions led to many depressive thoughts. In times like those, I realized that if I allowed one person's angst to create the same angst in me, I have allowed the enemy of my soul a secondary victory—and that victory taints my future.

As you project who you want to be in the future, perseverance is important. And in that act of persevering through relational trial, you are likely to butt up against an all-or-nothing mind-set. This happens when you make one small error, but you catastrophize it into the biggest mistake of your life. This pervasive thinking then causes you to give up entirely. It's all or nothing. You're either 100 percent perfect in the way you approach friendships and relationships, or you're an utter failure. Neither is true.

And therein lies a story. I'm finishing this book around

Christmastime. Nearly every day, I walk with my dog, Daisy, to our little park. One of the things that delighted me was this: Some anonymous Christmas elves had decorated a Charlie Brown Christmas tree in our woods. Decked out with glass balls, the tree reminded me of what is good about folks. But one day I noticed all the balls had been taken off the tree and smashed beneath it.

I could have given in to the idea that everyone is a hoodlum and no good people exist, but that is not the truth. There are noble folks too. A few days later, I noticed the tree had been redecorated. But as Daisy and I walked by it, another truth emerged. What if the secret elves allowed the vandals to win? What if they shook their heads, then believed their act of kindness meant nothing? First of all, regardless of what they did next (redecorate the tree), it didn't negate the beauty that they created. Second, because they persevered, more people were blessed.

All that to say, do not lose heart. Keep moving. If one difficult friend sidelines you, don't let that stop you from pursuing a safe friend. Paul reminds us, "So let's not get tired of doing what is good. At just the right time we will reap a harvest of blessing if we don't give up" (Galatians 6:9). And consider this: Double the people were blessed because the secret elves kept giving. They didn't allow a temporary setback to influence their behavior.

Spiritual growth is less about being perfect and more about your dependence on God in your stops and starts. Don't give up. Keep decorating your tree. Don't let the vandals win. Instead, be purposefully defiant! The best revenge is your joyful life—a life where you are no longer sidelined by other people's behavior.

Forward-thinking believers become what I call a *storyceiver* (story receiver). They let their past trauma make them empathetic. Instead of living in the land of lament and rehashing old arguments, they take all that pain and ask God to transform bitterness into empathy.

That empathy then empowers them to listen to other people's stories and offer kindhearted wisdom.

One of the most pivotal things happened in my own life when a friend of mine made an observation about me in my twenties. Scott rightly diagnosed me with an overactive conscience. His words didn't wound me. Instead they inspired me to seek help. We have the beautiful opportunity to be like Scott in other people's lives. Because of all we've learned on this journey of broken relationships, we can listen to the pain laced through people's stories, offering wisdom and insight for them. This is how the kingdom of God, that great forward momentum movement, brings us great joy. We are hurt, yes. But when Jesus intersects that hurt and heals us, we then become his agents of healing in a traumatized world. This, in a way, brings deeper meaning to our past relational pain because it becomes the catalyst to change many people's lives.

People who are forward bent are wholly expectant. They make room in their hearts for the creativity of God—even in seemingly impossible relationships. They allow him to complete the story in his way. God will do what you least expect. He specializes in doing *new* things. Instead of trying to orchestrate your own way, let God do what he wants in that toxic relationship. Sometimes that means a complete break off where you have the space to finally heal. Sometimes God ushers in reconciliation in relationships you never thought would heal. Sometimes it means giving you the grace to let go of marginal friendships so you have more emotional space for vital friendships.

Often in our prayer lives, we dictate to God how we want him to answer. We think we know how and when someone should repent or reconcile. We are humans. We do not have the eternal perspective of God, who is weaving stories we're unaware of. So let the Creator of all relationships be wildly creative in your midst.

Forward-thinking Christians project way into the future, and doing this empowers them to deal with difficult people today. Luke 20:36 reveals an important truth: Jesus said, "They will never die again. In this respect they will be like angels. They are children of God and children of the resurrection." When I get discouraged about the state of some of my deadly friendships, I look to the heavens, realizing someday there will be no more tears, no more angst, no more pain between me and other people. They will be perfectly realigned, living their best selves, no longer held back by their sinful patterns. Of course, I can't guarantee they'll be walking the streets of gold, but that is not my decision or prerogative. Viewing difficult people as children of resurrection has spurred me on, kept me joyful and expectant.

Let's revisit one of the scriptures I've highlighted from Psalm 1. The psalmist speaks of people who have learned to navigate difficult relationships. Of them he says, "They are like trees planted along the riverbank, bearing fruit each season. Their leaves never wither, and they prosper in all they do" (Psalm 1:3). That's my prayer for you—that you would bear fruit in each and every season, even in the winter season of toxic friendships.

My heart in writing this book is to bless you with evergreen thinking, to help you thrive even when temperatures drop or soar. You no longer need to be held hostage by broken relationships. Why? Because Jesus will empower you. He understands your pain. He walks alongside you in the midst of it. And he loves to renew us. He is the God of the resurrection, the one who called forth a once-dead Lazarus, the One who makes all things new. As we look to the end of time, we see this promise of trees and fruit and seasons come to fruition: "Then the angel showed me a river with the water of life, clear as crystal, flowing from the throne of God and of the Lamb. It flowed down the center of the main street. On each side of the river grew a tree of life, bearing twelve crops of fruit, with a fresh crop each month. The leaves were used for medicine to heal the nations" (Revelation 22:1-2). What a poignant picture of resurrection and life! Let's keep this in mind as we navigate our friendships today. Someday all things will be made new.

But what about today? Yes, it's important to look to the future, to live lives that promote better future relationships. But you picked up this book because you're currently hurting. What then? It's my sincere prayer that you'll experience hope now.

When I got married, one of the things Patrick said to me was this: "I want the second half of your life to be better than your first half." What he meant by that: He recognized the pain I'd experienced, but he also longed for me to find wholeness and health every day. I can honestly say my life has been so full of blessings and new relationships. Yes, I've struggled. Yes, I've been hurt by all seven of the deadly friendships. Yes, I've experienced heartache. But I've also seen the hand of God take all that mess and make a message of it— that we don't have to be held hostage to words and actions of others. Even Job experienced the kind of restoration my husband hinted at: "So the LORD blessed Job in the second half of his life even more than in the beginning" (Job 42:12).

The word I'll finish with is this: *feasting*.

Feasting doesn't seem to fit with deadly friendships. A good feast involves only joyful reverie with people we love. We see this when Job experienced a relational and material restoration: "Then all his brothers, sisters, and former friends came and feasted with him in his home" (Job 42:11). But in one of the most famous psalms, we see an echo of a different kind of feast: "You prepare a feast for me in the presence of my enemies. You honor me by anointing my head with oil. My cup overflows with blessings" (Psalm 23:5). The feast didn't come in the midst of happy friendships; it came while enemies shared the same table and food—and yet there are blessings. We see this play out in Jesus's life at the Passover supper before his betrayal and crucifixion. He literally dined with those who would desert and betray him—the deadliest of friends. Yet he feasted. He poured himself out. He fed his friends, washed their feet, prayed over them. He provided comfort, all the while knowing that in a few short hours, their sins would be forced upon his back. If he can feast in the midst of that kind of strife, we can too.

So my prayer for you as you close this book is this: May you be feasting.

Acknowledgments

I'm grateful (though I've not always been, to be honest) for the deadly friendships I've encountered throughout the years. They've caused me to look inward, assess my own poor tendencies, and simultaneously seek Jesus for healing. Using my branding terminology, they've been part of my re-story process.

I'm particularly grateful for my Writing Prayer Circle who have prayed for me more than 14 years now—all of whom are faithful friends. Thank you, Kathi, Sandi, Holly, Renee, Caroline, Cheramy, Jeanne, D'Ann, Darren, Dorian, Erin, Helen, Katy G., Katy R., Anita, Diane, Cyndi, Leslie, Liz, Rebecca, Sarah W., Tim, Tina, Nicole, Tosca, TJ, Patrick, Jody, Susan, Becky S., Dena, Carol, Susie, Christy, Alice, Randy, Paul, Jan, Thomas, Judy, Aldyth, Sue, Brandilyn, Lisa, Richard, Michele, Yanci, Cristin, Roy, Michelle, Ocieanna, Denise, Heidi, Kristin, Sarah V., Phyllis, Emilie, Lea Ann, Boz, Patricia, Anna L., Kendra, Gina, Ralph, Sophie, Anna S., Jodie, Hope, Ellen, Lacy, Tracy, Susie May, Becky B., Paula, John, Julie, Dusty, Tabea, Jessica, Cheri, Shelley, Elaine, Ally, and Amy. Any success in terms of the kingdom comes on the shoulders of your prayers.

Thank you to David and Sarah Van Diest, who have become sweet champions of my work.

I'm particularly thankful for the excellent publishing team at Harvest House. I'm grateful for Bob Hawkins Jr. and his genuine belief in my books. Thank you, Kathleen Kerr, for empowering my voice and catching my foibles. Sherrie Slopianka, thank you for being a terrific cheerleader and taking risks on me. I so appreciate you, Jessica Ballestrazze, for your keen marketing vision and your many creative ideas. Thanks, Christianne Debysingh, for your particular zeal for this book. And Ken Lorenz? You've become more than my salesman friend. You are a gem—fatherlike and utterly encouraging. Betty Fletcher, thank you for making the final product sing! Thanks, too, to Kyler Dougherty for the cover design—I love what you've done.

I'm indebted to my husband, Patrick, who always makes me laugh, and my three adult children, Sophie, Aidan, and Julia, who love me well. I'm less grateful for Daisy, our sock-stealing chocolate lab, who is insistent on making me into a dog person, but she is growing on me—slowly.

Jesus, you are my best friend. You never leave me nor forsake me. You teach me how to love all sorts of folks—even myself. Thank you for daring to call me your friend. I'm stunned.

Notes

Why You Need This Book

1. Shawn R. Tucker, *The Virtues and Vices in the Arts: A Sourcebook* (Eugene, OR: Cascade Books, 2015), 4.

2. Henry Cloud, *Necessary Endings: The Employees, Businesses and Relationships that All of Us Have to Give Up in Order to Move Forward* (New York: Harper Collins, 2010), 12.

3. Frederick Buechner, *Telling Secrets: A Memoir* (New York: HarperCollins, 1991), 30.

Chapter One—Narcissist Nolan

1. Shahida Arabi, "5 Sneaky Things Narcissists Do to Take Advantage of You," *Thought Catalog*, August 6, 2014, http://tcat.tc/XDPPnP.

2. Craig Malkin, "5 Early Warning Signs You're with a Narcissist," *Psychology Today*, June 21, 2013.

3. As quoted to Shahida Arabi, *Power: Surviving and Thriving After Narcissistic Abuse* (Brooklyn, NY: Thought Catalog Books, 2017), 34.

4. Diane Langberg, Twitter post, December 13, 2017, 7:00 a.m., https://twitter.com/Diane Langberg/status/940929357903749121.

5. Craig Malkin, "Can Narcissists Change?" *Psychology Today*, September 20, 2013, https://www .psychologytoday.com/blog/romance-redux/201309/can-narcissists-change.

Chapter Three—Predator Paige

1. All traits above from my article "13 Surprising Traits of Predatory People That You Might Just Overlook," *FaithIt.com*, December 29, 2016, https://faithit.com/13-signs-predatory-people-mary -demuth/.

2. Shahida Arabi, "Dating Emotional Predators: Signs to Watch Out For," *Self Care Haven*, August 29, 2014, https://selfcarehaven.wordpress.com/2014/08/29/dating-emotional-predators-signs-to-look -out-for/.

3. Ibid.

4. I recommend *The Sociopath Next Door* by Martha Stout, and *Predators* by Anna C. Salter.

5. "How to Handle the Religious Sociopath," VirtueOnline.org, July 27, 2007, http://virtueon line.org/how-handle-religious-sociopath.

6. Ibid.

Chapter Four—Conman Connor

1. David Modic, as quoted in Colin Barras, "How Con Artists Trick Your Mind," BBC.com, October 3, 2014, http://www.bbc.com/future/story/20141003-the-mind-tricks-of-scammers.

2. Ibid.

3. Maria Konnikova, *The Confidence Game: Why We Fall for It Every Time* (New York: Penguin Books, 2017), 49.

4. Ibid., 48.

5. Rachel Pavlik, "3-D Lashes, Jamberry & Other Ways to Lose Facebook Friends," *Scary Mommy* (blog), accessed February 12, 2018, http://www.scarymommy.com/how-to-lose-facebook-friends/.

6. Kate Shellnut, "Why Your Facebook Feed Is Filled with Women Selling Essential Oils and Press-On Nails," Vox.com, November 3, 2016, https://www.vox.com/2016/5/12/11577466 /multilevel-marketing.

7. "Multilevel Sales Programs," Crown.org, March 12, 2012, https://www.crown.org/multilevel -sales-programs/.

8. "What to Expect from Narcissistic People When They Get Old," Flying Monkeys Denied (blog), November 27, 2015, http://flyingmonkeysdenied.com/2015/11/27/expect-aging-narcissists-people -aspd/.

CHAPTER FIVE—TEMPTER TREVOR

1. Carolyn Hax, "Instagram Reveals Friends Traveled Without Her," SeattlePI.com, November 19, 2017, https://www.seattlepi.com/lifestyle/advice/article/Carolyn-Hax-Instagram-reveals-her-friends -went-12356813.php.

2. Tonya L. Chartrand and John A. Bargh, "The Chameleon Effect: The Perception-Behavior Link and Social Interaction," *Journal of Personality and Social Psychology* 76, no. 6 (1999): 893-910, https://acmelab.yale.edu/sites/default/files/1999_the_chameleon_effect.pdf.

3. Carlin Flora, "Bad Friends," *Aeon,* December 12, 2016, https://aeon.co/essays/when-a-friendship -turns-sour-more-than-feelings-get-hurt.

CHAPTER SIX—FAKER FIONA

1. Chamath Palihapitiya, as quoted in Julia Carrie Wong, "Former Facebook Executive: Social Media Is Ripping Society Apart," *The Guardian*, December 12, 2017, https://www.theguardian .com/technology/2017/dec/11/facebook-former-executive-ripping-society-apart.

2. Charles C. Dike, "Pathological Lying: Symptom or Disease?" *Psychiatric Times* 25, no. 7, June 1, 2008, http://www.psychiatrictimes.com/articles/pathological-lying-symptom-or-disease.

CHAPTER EIGHT—JOSEPH

1. Andrew Wilson, "The Best Retelling of the Jesus Story Isn't from Narnia or Harry Potter," *Christianity Today,* October 20, 2017, http://www.christianitytoday.com/ct/2017/november/best -retelling-jesus-story-narnia-harry-potter.html.

CHAPTER TEN—THE SEVEN LIFE-GIVING PRACTICES

1. Shahida Arabi, *Power: Surviving and Thriving After Narcissistic Abuse* (Brooklyn, NY: Thought Catalog Books, 2017), 192.

2. Ibid., 125.

3. Ibid.

4. Dick Foth, *Known: Finding Deep Friendships in a Shallow World* (Colorado Springs, CO: Water-Brook, 2017), 34.

5. Ibid., 35.

6. Steven F. Maier and Martin E.P. Seligman, "Learned Helplessness: Theory and Evidence," *Journal of Experimental Psychology: General* 105, no. 1 (1976): 4, doi: 10.1037/0096-3445.105.1.3.

7. Henri Nouwen, *Intimacy* (San Francisco, CA: HarperSanFrancisco, 1981), 23.

8. Mary DeMuth, *Not Marked: Finding Hope and Healing after Sexual Abuse* (Dallas, TX: Uncaged Publishing, 2013), 62-63.

9. Shannon Thomas, *Healing from Hidden Abuse* (Southlake, TX: MAST Publishing House), 137.

About the Author

Mary DeMuth is a writer, speaker, and podcaster who loves to help people live re-storied lives. Author of more than 35 books, including Christian living titles, Southern fiction, and her latest devotional entitled *Jesus Every Day*, Mary speaks around the country and the world. She is the wife of Patrick and the mom of three adult children. Find out more at MaryDeMuth.com.

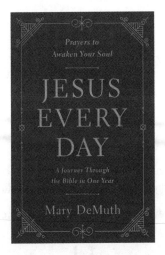

Jesus Every Day

Share Your Heart with the One Who Keeps It

Trying to juggle all your worries and burdens alone? As the challenges of everyday life threaten to continually distract you, your conversations with God can start to feel threadbare—too rushed to touch on the real issues that crowd your heart.

Rediscover your compassionate Savior with this collection of daily heart-provoking prayers and accompanying Scriptures from author and speaker Mary DeMuth. Each reading will awaken your tired soul, prompt new ways to encounter Jesus, and inaugurate the kind of authentic conversation you've always yearned to have with him.

Allow these daily prayers to release your hopes, worries, desires, and uncertainties to your Savior and find needed restoration and peace in his relentless grace. As you approach Jesus with a humble and honest spirit, you will discover how his mercy can absolutely change your life—today and every day.

To learn more about Harvest House books and
to read sample chapters, visit our website:

www.harvesthousepublishers.com

HARVEST HOUSE PUBLISHERS
EUGENE, OREGON